Utmost

Utmost

Two Physicians Share Their Experiences Serving Humanity During Disasters

Ashis Brahma, MD
Elizabeth A. Garcia-Janis, MD

Utmost: Two Physicians Share Their Experiences Serving Humanity During Disasters

Published by Wheatmark®
1760 East River Road, Suite 145
Tucson, Arizona 85705 USA
www.wheatmark.com

ISNB: 978-1-60494-271-2 (paperback)
ISNB: 978-160494-971-1 (ebook)
LCCN: 2009925016

rev201501
rev202002

Contents

Contents

Dear readers,

For your convenience, each letter written by Liz is prefaced by this symbol:

And each letter written by Ashis is prefaced by this symbol:

Foreword

About two years ago I met a life-loving and dynamic pair of humanitarians who share both their stories and their innermost realities on these pages: Liz first, through a mutual friend, then Ashis a few months later when he buzzed through my town on his way to a speaking tour destination, making time on the way for a coffeehouse interlude because we both trusted Liz's instinct that we would like each other.

I've met and written about many exceptional people—Oscar winners, Hall of Fame professional athletes, stadium-filling music stars. These two are standouts in my experience. Not because of their fame in humanitarian circles, though they deserve it, but because of the truth they've lived, the very direct connection of what they do with their lives to their passionate belief structures. Their concept of "utmost" emerges from a vibrant, shared willingness to place themselves on the front lines anytime they can alleviate suffering. Especially among the least powerful and the most hard-hit citizens of the world.

Here is what will last with me, the real benefit of being chosen to help edit the book Liz and Ashis wrote piece by piece, as they navigated the unexpected blossoming of a deeply personal relationship, along with a few disasters and emergencies, both third world and stateside: Throughout our lives, all of us are going to find ourselves on the front lines, over and over again. All of us will need to deal frequently with the setbacks and tragedies that strike both those we love and our own shaken selves. These events will test us all to the core.

Between the lines of their intertwined stories, you will begin to sense the great feelings, personal healing, friendships, and other rich experiences that flow when someone stretches to do his or her utmost for other people who suffer.

Utmost defines their way of relating to the world's needs. Your grasp of it will accumulate gradually from the stories these authors tell and the inward glances they share. Both the tellers and their tales will find a lasting place in your imagination.

I think you'll also experience a kind of emotional momentum in this book. It may warm your heart, but much more essentially it may show you something surprising—that any personal limitations you've felt while attempting to bring your inmost beliefs and the course of your life into alignment are probably not so difficult as you once thought them to be. That there's less distance between you and a beautiful dedication to your own utmost.

Utmost began from a free-associating, wide-ranging, and passionate personal correspondence between its two authors, a pair of multicultural doctors. One is a man, an MD of both Indian and Dutch descent, who discovered a calling to help throughout

Africa. The other is a woman, a psychiatrist born in the Philippines of mixed Filipino, Spanish, and Chinese bloodlines, trained in Europe, who has worked throughout an honors-laden career in an American heartland city, and yet also found herself providing post-disaster healing in Africa, Asia, and the Americas. You'll notice in places that their use of English can veer slightly from that of a native speaker (not surprising; they both speak a number of languages, and that's a lot of syntax to keep track of), though their intelligence and compassion always shine through, and so does the quirk that they love giving each other nicknames (which is a favorite social custom of Filipinos).

Between them, they've served in Chad (one extensively enough to be featured in a *60 Minutes* segment that won an Emmy), in Zimbabwe, in Thailand after the great tsunami, in the Philippines after the eruption of Mount Pinatubo, in Houston after Katrina, and in several other times of human need around the world.

They didn't start out with the idea of writing a book; they were simply celebrating and finding joy in their brand-new yet soulful, deep, and still growing mutual love, through a wish to share their frontline experiences in disaster relief, both from the recent past and the bullet-dodging present.

This celebration gradually helped them realize exactly why their emotional connection bloomed so instantaneously, and become so deeply loving. And that got them thinking that there was something in their letters that was worth sharing with you.

Ashis and Liz bonded because of their mutual dedication to humanitarian aid, just like soldiers who have ventured into battles together, each watching and worrying over the other's safety and well-being, becoming confidants to an extent that is beyond words, and certain to last as long as they live (at least).

Utmost

The words that fill their letters somehow, in a roundabout way, also richly evoke the kinds of feelings that usually exist beyond words, and somehow make palpable how powerfully volunteer service affects the life and spirits of the person who puts her- or himself on the line. Meanwhile, Liz (known more formally as Dr. Elizabeth Garcia-Gray and is currently Dr. Elizabeth Garcia-Janis) never knew what kinds of answers would result from sharing her thoughts with Ashis (Dr. Ashis Brahma), and he knew even less about how she might respond to his unpredictable flights of incident and emotion.

But the individual pieces of their interchange built themselves, in an organic way, into a whole that seems far more than the sum of its parts. It echoes a great truth: that as we pass through the harshness of life, we've got to know and remain connected to what keeps us sacred—which for these two remarkable and remarkably human people is love, friendship, brotherhood, and sisterhood, all relationships that are upholding of one another.

Welcome to *Utmost*, and to the inner reaches of two unforgettable hearts. I hope these stories serve you well.

—Byron Laursen, editor

Preface

Dear Reader,

Thank you, deeply, for your heartwarming interest in our book *Utmost*. For me, life has been a daily learning experience of how to give compassion and how to love more. My heart brims with gratitude in humbly being granted the opportunity to live each beautiful moment of life to the utmost. The way we live our lives and the way we respond to life's circumstances are our innermost choices.

Many of us, at some point in our lives, will experience life challenges that can put us to the edge of life and the unknown. Each one of us will respond to our many trials the best we can. Some of us may even feel that we are walking that tightrope between life and death, depending on what we are experiencing. We take daily risks in responding to what life gives us. We realize that

Utmost

we do not have complete control over life's tribulations and the Universal Plan, so we fall back to walking in profound faith.

Dr. Ashis Brahma and I were brought together by our personal and spiritual missions, right in the heart of Africa. From there we exchanged stories about our humanitarian experiences and our thoughts and feelings about humanity and how to give our utmost to the world. We easily became the closest friends, feeling like we were comrades-in-arms in serving those who suffer disasters, losses, and tragedies.

The last couple of years of our lives have given us a glimpse of the mystery behind the meaning of soul-friendship, unconditional love for family and friends, love of God and mankind. We also learn more each day about how our many foibles, perceived frailties, and weaknesses can grow into the very strengths that anchor our spirits, the concept of the Phoenix Miracle—those who rise from the ashes of despair to soar and give light and compassion to others.

We have included in this book many of our favorite quotes, old words of wisdom, and some prayers to share the simplicity of what helped keep our minds grounded during the most chaotic times in our disaster work. In the midst of chaos, we can be helped by focusing our minds on prayer, meditation, the beauty of nature, and simple serene words that create a blanket of peace within our souls. Some of the stories about the patients we cared for were blended to protect their privacy, and names were not mentioned and/or have been changed.

I thank Dr. Ashis Brahma, my dear friend and co-author; Byron Laursen, our friend and content editor, for his support and his loving encouragement; and Marissa, my brilliant and talented sister and dearest friend; and our many global humanitarian friends for making this book a miraculous reality.

My gratitude goes to Hayley Love, our editor at Wheatmark, for her professionalism and dependable consistency.

My love goes to my huge extended family, especially my children, Alex and Jacqueline, for being my best teachers about life and unconditional love.

I am grateful to God for Lawrence and his wonderful extended family. Love does come to those of us who believe in its mystery.

I dedicate this book to all the people who trusted me to be their physician. Thank you for teaching me compassion.

It is with humility, gratitude, and love that our book is presented to you. May you give your utmost in your daily life to experience the power of your compassion and love.

With love,
"Liz"
Elizabeth A. Garcia-Janis, MD

Dear Reader,

Utmost is a journey and a dialogue between two physicians, Dr. Elizabeth Garcia-Janis and Dr. Ashis Brahma. I am Ashis. My portion of the dialogue was inspired by experiences that I encountered while working in the Oure Cassoni refugee camp in eastern Chad, and on my later return to Chad to launch a foundation, lecture at a university, and work in a hospital in Bebedja.

Utmost

During these two times in the field I was robbed, mugged, shot at by rebel forces, bombed by airplanes, and essentially lived under prison-like circumstances for security reasons. Elizabeth has worked in the aftermath of several natural disasters, including Katrina and the devastating Asian tsunami. Our exchange began as a personal dialogue, but turned rather rapidly toward addressing some existential issues of devoting oneself to service of others: What is utmost? Why do people put themselves on the line, committing all the personal and professional resources they can, and enjoy it?

Blogging gave me the hang of the writing process, but *Utmost* is my first attempt at writing a book. It has led both of us to tackle yet another book, which we have determined will be called *Be*.

Given our natural aptitudes for spelling mistakes and typos, I am very grateful that Byron Laursen, a more experienced writer and editor, has gone through the document to make his magic work and help our voices to emerge.

Another love that Liz and I share is the Phoenix Global Humanitarian Foundation, to which all profits from this book shall proceed. Visit http://www.PGHF.org.

I dedicate this book to Peter Aalders, my friend, who is no longer with us.

With love,
"Ashis"
Ashis Brahma, MD

Interconnectedness

Rome—Addis Ababa, 8 November 2007

Right now I'm feeling connected to the past, yet loose, just letting my mind sift through some good memories.

My college fraternity will always be deep in my heart. I remember the day as if it was yesterday, when I finally became an alumnus after seven years of active membership. There are plenty of misconceptions about fraternities—superficial thoughts about the boozing, hazing, ogling, burping, farting, and all other factoids that are true. Once again I saw four young men choking back tears and ultimately crying because a next step in our lives was being taken. A standing ovation as their final letter was being read. Stories of "*himmelhoch jautzed und zum Tode betrubt*," which means in English "ecstatic joy and moribund sadness". Idiocy like a confederacy of dunces.

Even though there are age differences among the group, there is also the common stream of shared experiences. A fellow doctor, just then newly graduated, was invited to sleep over in the room above our fraternity bar. He had not yet become a surgeon. Different times but same, same. Always out to create mischief and get the maximum out of life. A few years later he will go to Chad to help out, teaching Chadian doctors, despite taking a 150 thousand euro loan to finish his twelve-year specialization. Money does not matter. Living with a deep sense of gratitude that you do the max does.

I did my best to collect more of these fine people around me. Another fraternity member, another doctor. He will be going to India to do an internship at the Calcutta institute where I once worked.

My life is about finding the deep end, balancing at the edge and tumbling over. No fear to fall or fail. As all will be well in life. Trust in self will lead to accepting what is not meant to be and what will be possible. Trust in self will lead to memorable achievements in life. These are the concepts that I want to rule my life. Sometimes they seem to be only some words that I grab for, trying to understand my life and make it feel more stabilized. Sometimes it becomes easier to feel these truths, and to know that I really am living by them. Sometimes I feel them so certainly that they're like the air I breathe or the blood in my veins. These are some of the thoughts that I can often feel deeply.

Let go of pride. Utmost is doing without expecting respect, honor, monetary or any other kind of gain. Do according to talent and karma. Be balanced in joy about success, balanced about sadness from failure, balance in all and all.

Utmost within the human spirit lies the soul, a temple of

mental, spiritual, and physical strength. Remember the mother who lifts the car when her child lies underneath it. Or the inner strength refugees have after losing all.

Is it fear that keeps people holding back from reaching for the utmost?

The only thing we need to fear is fear itself.

Be the change you want to see in the world. Let your light shine as bright as it is. After all, sitting under the tree and closing your eyes gives the maximum of wisdom. Books lead to knowledge, but not to wisdom.

Talk with a child. Talk with your inner child. Talk with a senior. Listen to the trees. Listen to Nature. Trust your insights. Trust yourself only. Trust all. Embrace ambiguity. All of living is accepting the endless potential within. It all boils down to love. Love is all you need. Wisdom is overrated. Truth is never utmost. Truth is always relative. Love is always utmost. Love is the devotion to the divine. The interconnectedness. Different divine names are all the different ways to express the utmost. That which we cannot name is what we fear. That loving will lead to endless potential?

Liz, you are probably closest to the utmost I have ever seen any living being. Clearly mothers do not count in this equation, but your devotion to life and to helping other people is just like a mother's devotion to a child.

Utmost is seeing and feeling the humor in all. Krishna sets the golden example. Mischief is the utmost solution.

Louisville, Kentucky, USA. 10 November 2007

Fever. Muscles moaning to feel relief from malaise. Upper respiratory infection. Physician heal thyself. Better yet, physician rest.

Several of the children I saw at work today were ill. They came in, guilelessly and tenderly, ready to hug their doctor in their innocent playful ways. And I savored absorbing all those hugs. So I got the hug bug.

Children are our teachers in what utmost is about. They give. They take. Yet they give more. When children love, they love with every fiber of their being. And when they get mad, it is also with every fiber of their being.

Restless night. Doses of Tylenol lowered the temperature, but it was still hard to breathe. I felt like I was burning up. I had to think cool. Envision snow falling, see ocean waves. I finally broke into a sweat. My favorite red cotton pajamas soaked it all up. With my eyes closed so as not to interrupt my semi-sleep, I groped into the dark for a large cotton T-shirt. In the process, I started reminiscing.

Ashis, your love for your fraternity reminds me of my love for the Prepians. My high school friends. They remind me of where I came from. They remind me of my inner child and the need to nurture it. They remind me of the Philippines. The culture, traditions, the nuances of being a Filipino. Roots. Unconditional friendships.

Speaking of friends, one of them just called yesterday sharing his anxieties and sadness about a daughter who was reportedly suicidal. She told someone in school about her self-destructive thoughts. Consequently the police had to intervene to protect her from herself and she had to be hospitalized. I listened. I encouraged him and his family to seek help for themselves as well. There is an inner sense of devastation, powerlessness, and helplessness felt by a family when a family member becomes suicidal and/or homicidal. An enormous loving family is rich with both joys and sorrows. The benefits of the joys far outweigh the risks of the sorrows. Love even more when people are at their worst. Giving utmost love when it is hardest to give is a divine gift.

Then there was a phone call from a lady with a serious tone of voice. Her voice also sounded shaky, apprehensive. My heart fluttered a bit. I could sense that the next words from her mouth would be about a loss. Indeed. My sister-in-law's stepfather just died. I could not believe it. My heart felt so saddened, especially because I just lost my brother Jun a few weeks ago. What pain must my sister-in-law Elisa feel? To lose her beloved soul mate, her husband. And then to lose her stepfather, who was more than a father to her. A good, kind, and loving man.

Both my brother and my sister-in-law's stepfather died from heart attacks. Two good men with enormous hearts and compassion for so many. Two who have given their utmost to the families they loved more than their own lives. Do the good really die young?

I spoke with my sister-in-law and her mother. What more can I say except that I love them? Their deep sorrow traveled from the phone wires into my heart. How I wish I could take away people's pain.

Yet that same pain allows us to evolve and grow. The pain that enables us to cultivate our inner strength and depth of compassion and love. In recovery work they say, "Pain is inevitable; suffering is optional."

I am beginning to understand the meaning of this as my life unfolds. Having suffered pain does not mean that we stop feeling joy. It does not mean that we will not be open to new beginnings in our lives. It does not mean that we stop loving. For to suffer is to stop feeling all that is most precious in life. The joy. The peace. The compassion. The love.

You talk about fear. I fervently believe that the opposite of love is fear. The less fear, the more love. Love is like a cliffhanger. Do I jump? Do I jump now or later? Perhaps now *and* later.

My brother Jun certainly understood the meaning of fearlessness. He had no qualms about jumping right into whatever risks there might be, to defend and protect people the best he could. Are we able to love to the utmost if we don't have it within ourselves to lay our lives out for others? Is it a requirement for utmost love? Is this interpretation mainly coming from my understanding of what love means from Jesus Christ's standpoint?

Socrates is truly brilliant. The more we know, the more we don't know. I find solace in that thought. On the other hand, as human beings, we naturally have fears. Perhaps fearlessness is not the issue. Perhaps it is all about courage and acting in spite of fears, as Mark Twain said, "Courage does not mean the absence of fears." But then again, someone like Jun seemed fearless and courageous. What causes these inner fears that stop us from loving to our utmost? Do we even need to fear fear?

Your thoughts on pride are like pearls. Pride is a tough thing to let go. It is the last fortress for our human sense of control. A defense for our vulnerable psyche. Pride is a cover-up of our human weaknesses. And yet pride also holds some form of strength.

That lion-pride of being allows us to have that utmost esteem to go where others would not dare to go. The temperance of pride, that balance, is hopefully what we aim for so we can accomplish all that we need to do in this lifetime.

On trusting self. Is it the self we trust, or the spirit of the self? I find comfort in trusting in a power greater than myself. This does not mean that I do not trust my own intentions and actions. On a human level, if I can trust someone 90 percent of the time, chances are that person is trustworthy enough for me. The 90-10 principle also applies to my own self. However, I believe in the greater glory of the human being through a higher power. This way of thinking helps me comprehend our interconnectedness to the whole. Maybe the "and-and" principle works here as well. Trusting in the self *and* a higher power.

On wisdom. There is truly a difference between knowledge and wisdom. And we probably need both to direct us toward our life purpose. Nothing beats experiential learning in terms of assimilating what life has to teach us. I believe that the essence of our wisdom is already within us from the day we are born. What we learn in life is merely tapping into what is already embedded in our genetic coding and spiritual selves. That's why we sometimes meet young people who are like old souls. They seem to exude the wisdom of the ages.

Funny how someone recently told me that he felt I was a young soul. I suppose it just means I have so much more to learn in life, and this friend probably sensed my big child within.

I like learning from everyone and everything. I learn most from the children. They all keep us honest and loving.

And I do learn a lot from nature. The way that people have reacted to my book *Your Compassionate Nature* was a surprise to me. It's a book of photographs of serene and tranquil sunsets, sunrises, waterfalls, and beautiful nature, pictures I took during global disaster relief work, to serve as a contrast to the chaos, to help find the beauty that exists even in the midst of the tragedy. It is hard to believe that it is now published and has gone out into the public. My mental photographs, my memories of beautiful nature, help me access inner peace and strength during times of disaster or tragedies. This was not the book I planned to release first. It just goes to show you that we can plan all we want; Destiny has its whims.

We shall talk more about embracing ambiguity (something Leonardo da Vinci was known to be great at), about Truth and Love. And the endless potential of love is well expressed by William Shakespeare:

> *My bounty is as boundless as the sea*
> *My love as deep, the more I give to thee*
> *The more I have*
> *For both are infinite.*

Based on Krishna's example, how do we integrate humor, mischief, and love? Is love about giving our utmost? Just maybe, we are each other's spiritual mirrors in our desire to give the world our utmost.

Miss you back.

14 November 2007

Today was one of those days that my mind wandered off to contemplate and appreciate the infinite beauty of one single moment. In a second, or what I thought was a second, I had a memory flash of my two children happily playing on a beach in Jamaica with other little children. The Boscobel all-inclusive resort had what they called "super-nannies," local women who taught the children all kinds of water sports. The kids also got to build adorable sandcastles, and they even learned to dance the limbo. To hear my children's laughter, to see the joy in their faces, to feel their delight was beyond precious in that extraordinarily special snapshot in time. I carry that picture inside of me wherever I go. My daughter was running around the beach with the biggest smile on her face, telling me about the "free ice cream cones" they were giving out to the children. Utmost delight.

Now we go to fast-forward. A stark contrast. My work with our community refugees teaches me the meaning of inner strength and resilience in children. The nine-year-old child of a refugee from Sudan talked to me today about losing his father, grandparents, and his aunts. He remembers his home burning. He remembers shots. He remembers being pushed and shoved. He remembers dead people. Nightmares of the past still plague him. Now he is in America with his mother and sister.

In school, some kind teachers have gone out of their way to help him adjust. He is coping in his own way. I like the way he smiled when he told me that now he has a best friend. And that they enjoy playing basketball. There was that same moment of infinite beauty that I saw in my kids' faces in Jamaica showing in the boy's face as he narrated how he got the ball in the basket just in time for his team to win. The light in his eyes. That same delight my daughter had. Children of such diverse backgrounds, yet that same joy. Dealing with life to their utmost as life gives it to them. Moment by moment. Day by day.

Why must I be thinking about all this now? Are not all children our children? Are not all parents our parents?

Are we not all one?

Spiritual Success

November 2007

Maximize the quest for understanding; maximize the joy; maximize the intensity.

As long as I can remember it has been like this. If there is a rule to be found, explore the boundary, jump over it, and accept the consequences. Without surpassing rules and regulations, true understanding does not appear easily to me. Experience is required.

What are boundaries? Social conventions invented by people to regulate society? Logical natural behavior? Dogma dictated?

To reach utmost, self needs to disappear. Not because character without self will lead to fame, respect, the moral high route, but because without desire and lust these needs remain: universal love and service.

Liz, our chat today made me realize how egoistic I have been. Why I end up time and time again in the same soup. I do not fear a path of celibacy. In fact a path of physical, mental, and spiritual health is much more interesting. Being in utmost form will lead to utmost result. Gosh, how great is it to be top fit like a race-horse? I am finding back my mental and spiritual balance. Now let the physical follow, turn into a black belt yogi Zen master. You know, I am being inspired to eat more vegetarian here. When I have a kitchen, I shall cook veg and fish only.

Chad is in my life to teach me cha(d)stity. Regain the patience point. Turn to teaching and writing. Lead a visionary mission. Know it will utterly succeed. I am re-finding the utmost self. Dust off the distraction. Focus on the success.

Road Runner, we are going to fly.

Cannot wait to see you.

15 November 2007

Success. What is it anyway, my Mr. Blowfish? Many times in my life, what I thought was success turned out to be the peak of a developmental spiritual cycle. I stand at the mountaintop of what I had always dreamed of during that time, and then I look at everything around me. All that has been done. All that has been accomplished. All that has been accumulated. So much. Then this irrational angst hits me. Existential. And spiritual. That restlessness known only by the soul that innately longs to grow and evolve. Then gradually, another spiritual growth cycle within a lifetime of lifetimes sprouts up.

There shall be many mountain peaks for us. Even within a lifetime. Standing up there at what we perceive is at the apex of living gives us a chance to understand the meaning of letting go of it all. No different from an innocent little child happily building his blocks. And after he has built the blocks tall enough for his satisfaction, what does he do? He joyfully knocks it all down and laughs and smiles proudly. And then what? He builds another block tower. Taller and more balanced than before.

Success has taken on a different meaning for me. It is immersed in that everyday knowing that our hearts are in a momentum to do good for many. It is not so hidden in the souls of two people who will go to the maximum of giving their best love and compassion for the world. It is in that acceptance that success is because of the All and not necessarily the one. Ralph Waldo Emerson said it well:

"To laugh often and much; to win the respect of intelligent people and the affection of children; to earn the appreciation of honest critics and endure the betrayal of false friends; to appreciate beauty; to find the best in others; to leave the world a bit better, whether by a healthy child or a garden patch ... to know that one life has breathed easier because you have lived. This is to have succeeded." I dare add that to succeed is to be able to love to our utmost in the best way we know how.

On egoism. I think as we evolve, we need a certain sense of healthy egoism to define ourselves, to make our mark in our universe.

However, it helps to remember that we are all more than our

egoism. And we are all more than what we perceive are our successes and failures. And we are way more than any of our illnesses. Just my take, but it always feels true to me.

There is something profound in being able to face our own dragons. Facing our dragon-shadow takes courage and eventually eliminates all fear after one is able to look the dragon right in the eye. And furthermore, just imagine befriending that dragon. Taming it enough so we can cohabitate with it in harmony. Realizing full well that the dragon is an integral part of our very soul. So how can we use our egotistical drives to some good? Or is the egoism merely a perception and a judgment on the self? Egoism for some may well be great self-esteem for another. Balance. And most of all discernment.

I was also contemplating about our Skype chat. Many times, in people's desire to make good things happen, we both know that the goodness within us has to face the many challenges, distractions, and obstacles that come our way. Some people may interpret the things we do in disheartening ways. Others will refuse to believe that a lot of good can actually be done in this world. From the simplest random act of kindness to risking one's life to save many. We may even be called every name in the book for doing what we believe is the right thing.

Our goal is to keep our focus on our missions and not allow anyone or anything to poison our hearts with venomous negativity. Not even our own. Principles over personalities. We cannot please the whole world no matter what we do. Jesus Christ is God to many, and he was flagellated and tortured. Buddha coped by detaching himself. Mother Theresa and Gandhi were criticized and ridiculed in their desire to be the changes they wanted to see in the world. Who are we not to be ridiculed, judged, and maligned by other fellow human beings? It does not mean we condone those behaviors either. We have no control and are powerless over what others say and do. So what they say and do about us is really none of our business. We have no control over others. So what do we do? We pray for others. We pray for the world and ourselves. We meditate to harmonize all our spirits into One. We focus on those who give love and encouragement to help us along our paths, and think of the distractions as challenges for our spirits. We access the utmost part of ourselves to give love to the unlovable. Our favorite Gilbert K. Chesterton quote: "To love is to love the unlovable."

How true. And how utmost is this concept. Even if we, ourselves, may sometimes be the unlovable.

On food. Eating a not-too-strict vegetarian diet is great! And when are you cooking the gourmet meals you promised me, may I ask? Veggies and fish and rice. I can live with that. Oh, and tomatoes, please.

Celibacy. Oh my! Nothing to fear. After the withdrawals, smooth sailing. ;) Lots of suppressed and pent-up sexual and sensual energies can be beautifully transformed to help and serve many in our world. Increased creativity and sense of inner peace. The Tantric masters know this secret well. It is no coincidence that many who take the spiritual path stay celibate. A conservation of energy. A preservation of the purity of spirit. A symbol of surrendering the flesh.

Nowadays, reckless sexual interactions can be deadly. I want to uplift the essence of Life. Sexuality and sensuality are precious gifts and do not need to be misused or abused. Loving one man to the maximum, giving of myself to one man, a man I love very deeply, for the rest of my life, with all the ups and downs, that would be an utmost gift. Our past relationships, our past loves have taught us a lot. I am learning that being loved back is not necessary anymore, even though it is warmly appreciated. Being loved back is optional. Although a mutuality doubles the joy of loving.

Rules. There are human rules and there are higher rules. And some crossover. Rules are not so antagonistic if interpreted as mere guidelines or concepts that help facilitate some semblance of order and structure to prevent havoc. They have their significance for the whole. Human rules only become truly problematic when they become so rigid that people start to forget the humanity of others. This is when higher rules prevail. In disaster work, refugee work, and helping save lives, as you already know, many human rules are thrown to the side for the higher rules. Whatever it takes to help save one life is the thrust. We have both been in those situations many times.

On boundaries. To keep it simple, I like to visualize a healthy cell. A healthy cell has a semipermeable membrane. The membrane is not a wall. And it is not amorphous. It releases the toxins. It absorbs the nutrients. So it is with each human being to another. Neither walled-off nor fused. Hugging is humanizing. Tender. Loving. With mutual consent it feeds our hearts and souls with joy. I like to cross boundaries that divide us from one another. And I like to maintain boundaries so that we do not dissolve into each other's oblivion.

Like Kahlil Gibran so beautifully explained: "let there be spaces in your togetherness and let the winds of the heavens dance between you … And stand together though not too near together;

for the pillars of the temple stand apart; and the oak tree and the cypress grow not in each other's shadow."

My thoughts? More free hugs for the world!

Wish we were working together right now, Ashis.

N'Djamena—17 November 2007

Dear Liz,

Success is enjoying the simplest moments and accepting self, yet at the same time striving to become yet more. It is as you said about the young Sudanese refugee in the USA. He now has a best friend and he enjoyed scoring the winning hoop in a basketball match. It reminds me of a team handball game long ago. Our opponents were evenly matched with us; perhaps they were slightly better. Always close matches. That particular game our team was one or two goals behind the whole match. Three consecutive attacks in the second half I received the ball. I played (if to compare with basketball as a center) in between the defense of the other team. Three times I tricked the guys around me and chucked the ball in the goal past the goalie. It ended up being our three final goals of the match. The final score was 11-11, a draw. There is peace in accepting you are equal as a team on a given day. The concept in the USA of sport is different, however. There must be a winner. I kind of like equilibrium. It gives a sense of liberation if you know as a team you have done your utmost to play your best game.

Back to the refugees in Chad. It is there that you see how

resilient humanity is, how much humor and how much dignity it has. After losing everything—and I am talking about burned houses, stolen cattle, raped women, murdered babies, executed men, getting called "abeed" (black slave), and chased from their hometowns, the Zaghawa I met were still occupied with arranging primary, secondary education for their kids. There were literacy classes for the women while in the refugee camp. Children playing with self-made hoops and mud car toys. *Laughing* as kids do.

It is when you put people through the ringer that you realize that there is a spirit that is not destructible. A hardcore utmost essence of human spirit. One that will not bow, will play and keep on moving despite. One that is always in the moment. Does not lament about yesterday, that does have a vision. But is today.

It is as it is today.

The 4x4 Toyota RAV is being prepared for our seven-hour drive to Mondou. It is there where I am sure to find work aplenty. Money will come flowing in somehow. It is a matter of jumpstarting the work without it. Good people come on your path when you want to do good. It may seem a platitude, but it is truth. I know of five groups of people and several individuals from around the world who will come to Chad to help with the little baby Africa Vision. Trusting everything will be all right. Africa teaches a lot. The most beautiful of lessons is patience. To accept that your way to the perceived top of a mountain may be a bumpy ride and that obstacles will come on your path.

By the way, your reference about standing on top of hills at times so much rings a bell. There have been times in my life where I thought, "Wow, I am cruising. Everything is going my way. I am on the peak of pleasure, success, and happiness." Mmmm, a nice thought to have. But truly I am realizing that every moment could be that moment of Zen peace as long as you truly do what you want, reflect on what that is, listen to others, trust your guts. It is never wrong that way. Yet be open to question that state of mind, body, and soul.

I have limited access to quotes and all, writing from my house, but as I do have Internet access I will weave in some of the wordsmith's hot thoughts.

Make Me an Instrument

18 November 2007

Your baby. Africa Vision. It requires a lot of attention, focus, and tender loving care, Ashis. I even love the name. Hopeful. Uplifting Africa. You shall be a great dad to this baby, undoubtedly. And it will be awesome to watch the baby grow and be robust and happy and serve the world in some way.

Your being in Chad again reawakens several memories. Flashbacks. I remember when we first touched base. That was only a little more than a year ago. Can you believe that? Feels like it's been years. Chad was clearly not in my plans. Not even meeting you. I was already scheduled to go to Uganda in February, so flying to Chad in December was definitely not in my conscious intentions. I first landed in Omidyar.net, a global humanitarian platform based on the belief that one person can make a difference, and that people can make good things happen in this world. Pierre and Pam Omidyar, the owners of eBay, founded the O-Net platform. It was a thought-provoking blog about ways to solve poverty that led me to their idealistic site. I met many bright, innovative, and interesting people there, from all over the globe, transcending racial, gender, religious, and socioeconomic boundaries.

I was hooked. And learned a whole lot. I became one of five people from different parts of the world creating a proposal for grants and fundraising and uplifting the Clean Water for the World cause, and that is how and why I ran across you. Another physician. Working with refugees whose cause is another of my passions. Humanitarian. Kindred spirits and missions.

We started to dialogue through O-Net. You shared a lot of your joys working with the refugees; your frustrations in dealing with the bureaucratic distractions and challenges; your angst about the insanity of four hundred thousand people dead in Darfur while the majority of the world looked away. And for you to be the only physician there for such a long period of time, taking care of twenty-six thousand refugees, got to me.

Backup is important to me. I remember times doing mission work when I wished I had some type of backup. Another physician who would allow me to rest a little bit for some relief so I could go ahead and serve more. And when you wrote me that the NGO in charge of taking care of the mental health of refugees was forced to evacuate, and you were left to take care of those patients, then I felt even more compelled to go there. Even two weeks of disaster relief work can help stabilize psychiatric acuity to some degree. And since I spoke a rusty French and Arabic, and had done disaster work globally, it seemed at the time that I would be a shoo-in to volunteer and help in whatever way possible, even if just for a short time. And during the holidays, many of the relief workers go home to get some decompression and respite.

At this point, I will enter the reflections of my trip to Chad that I blogged soon after coming back home:

Tuesday, 2 January 2007

N'Djamena, Chad, and the Sudan Crisis: Part 1

Lord, make me an instrument of your peace: where there is hatred, let me sow love; where there is injustice, pardon; where there is doubt, faith; where there is despair, hope; where there is dark, light; where there is sadness, joy."
                                    —St. Francis of Assissi, 1181–1226

Going with the flow was like a roller-coaster ride in deciding to go to Chad. I could not bear to visualize dying children in mothers' arms, women getting raped, more people getting tortured and killed. How can anyone even doubt that this is genocide? The Sudan crisis has now expanded into Chad and the Central African Republic. Most of the world is still just watching. Many are still unaware. And sadly, many are in heavy denial of what is happening because it has not reached their private backyards. During the last couple of weeks prior to December 23, 2006, I felt compelled to be in Chad to serve the refugees and give some relief to colleagues and other humanitarian workers in whatever way during the holidays. Whatever small service I can do. There are brothers and sisters out there who are suffering. This is a soul thing. My personal gift to my loved ones for Christmas.

The logistics changed—not only daily, but almost hourly. No plans could be made with any certainty. Miraculously, I actually got my visa on time and my Thuraya satellite phone a day before departure. Intensive immersion in the many articles and news about the Sudan crisis and the potentially explosive scenario in the refugee camps in Chad strengthened my decision to go. I also got backup coverage at work in such a short period of time.

I spoke with my family, my children, and they understood. Several members of our extended family do mission work, so even though they may not have liked my going to Chad, because of obvious safety risks, they still understood. Following what seems to be the right thing to do has always been good for my spirit.

The journey from Louisville to Cincinnati to Paris to N'Djamena was seamless and generally smooth. I thought about the refugees. The wish to hug them. The humanitarian workers who are most probably already beyond compassion fatigue and secondary stress. Finally, I arrived in N'Djamena almost close to midnight. The Aeroport International N'Djamena was somewhat old and run-down; it exemplified the difficult infrastructure of Chad. Whatever I remember of French and Arabic words started to gush in my mind. I focused auditorily on the languages being spoken all around me, almost to a dizzying level. And yet, something felt familiar. There were men who looked like soldiers and men who were wearing their long, flowing Arabic garb. It was hard to see at night and it was very disorienting. Someone called out my name and then handed me a piece of paper saying that my baggage was delayed. Okay, then.

I dragged my hand-carry luggage outside of the airport, and looked for a cab. There were no women out there, only men. They probably were wondering what in the world a woman was doing out there in the middle of the night, in a culture where women could certainly benefit from more empowerment. Especially in a country where the humanitarian workers like those from UN-HCR and IRC were being evacuated because of heightened security problems. Some humanitarian workers have been robbed, assaulted, and there were reports that some were killed.

At that time, I was too tired to be fearful. In my understanding, a situation like that was an opportunity to serve. Having done disaster work and global medical missions, knowing some basic conversational French and Arabic, familiar with the culture for having worked closely with the Sudanese and other African refugees in my community, and years of experience in ASD and PTSD work allowed me no decision except to go.

A man tried to help me with my baggage and redirected me toward several cab drivers. That I felt a bit uncomfortable, especially when they started talking at the same time and were haggling as to who would drive me to my hotel, was an understatement. I took a deep breath, decided to maintain my composure, and built up confidence to look at their eyes directly, and spoke some French-Arabic with two of them. One of them smiled when he heard Arabic and French words from me so I decided to trust and go with that cab driver. *Je parle un peu francais. Parlez vous anglais? Je ne sais pas. Vous etes bien aimable. Mar-haba. Kif halak? Shok-ran. Menfadlak ... S'il vous plait, monsieur, Hotel Le Meridien Chiari. Merci.*

Deep Gratitude

24 November 2007

Happy Thanksgiving

Good to be home with my dad, stepmom, and brother for Thanksgiving. Howie, our newly adopted brother, came along, which was great. He is working on getting into his psychiatric residency at the University of Louisville. We spent time practicing how to answer mock interview questions while driving to Terre Haute, Indiana. Dad appeared to be resilient. Missing my brother Jun. One of my main purposes in being here in Indiana is to be with Elisa, Jun's wife, and her mom, Shirley. How can we fathom losing a spouse and a father within one month? Yet then again, how can the Darfur refugees even absorb the meaning of losing several family members and friends all at the same time? From insane and random attacks from others. And for what reason?

Insanity cannot be analyzed. Love the unlovable. Yet make a stand to stop the unlovable actions. And how do people heal from natural disasters? Where their whole communities are literally wiped out as by the Southeast Asian tsunami? How do we remain grateful in devastating circumstances? Situations that test the limits of our tolerance of loss, despair, and pain?

Thanksgiving celebrations can stir mixed emotions that challenge our spirits, reminding us of the tragedies, losses, and disasters in our lives. And for those who know how to forgive, and give thanks and appreciation for their lives, now those for me are the healthy positive attitudes to have toward the utmost.

Many beautiful things in my life are connected with the Thanksgiving holiday.

Firstly, Jackie, my dear daughter, was born close to this holiday. And secondly, my paternal grandparents (Mamang and Papang) also had a Thanksgiving birthday. And a difficult thing also happened on this holiday. The bittersweet part of Thanksgiving for me was the tragedy with my son that led to his complicated situation of needing to learn to deal with a life cloistered from the world. How amazing that a tragedy can lead to learning about the utmost meaning of unconditional love, forgiveness, mercy, and grace.

My gratitude runs deeply. A thankfulness that no matter what the circumstance, the cup runneth over. For these tragedies teach us the true understanding of courage, forgiveness, and love. I am not entirely sure where this sense of gratitude comes from. From my family? Friends? Genetics? Not totally sure. All I know is that an utmost feeling like gratitude gives us a sense of our relativity to a power of our understanding that is greater than us.

Last night, my family and friends went to see a band. And we danced our hearts out and laughed all night. I thought about you while we were dancing, and remembered how in New York City we danced until we dropped. I remember us being somewhere in Greenwich Village, where it ended up that you and I were the only ones dancing. And then my feet started to hurt, and you were the only one left dancing. Dancing to our utmost. Simple pleasure of life.

Tonight we will be having a bonfire, and stay at my brother Brian's home. Marshmallow roasts. Making s'mores. Playing guitar and singing. My kind of thing to do with family and friends. Probably more dancing, too.

Again, back to memories of when I first met you in Chad. And I recall ending up getting stuck in the Meridien Hotel of N'Djamena. My suitcase, which was loaded with medical supplies for the Oure Cassoni refugee camp, was delayed six days. Guterres of UNHCR visited Chad around the time I was there and recommended that the humanitarian workers evacuate because of the seriousness of the dangers and lack of safety. Plane rides to Bahai were scarce. I had a lot of supplies that I thought could be used in the camp. I just had the clothes from a small carry-on. And if not able to go to the camp, I had a contact in N'Djamena working with orphaned children of AIDS where I could do a needs assessment. There was also the option of going with a group of French relief workers to the south of Sudan. I truly did not think I would meet you there, the way our schedules were. All I knew was that I was glad that you were on your way to Cameroon to rest, relax, and enjoy. I thought I would meet up with Gabriel and Stacey from the I-ACT StopGenocideNow.org. That seemed more probable at the time.

I arrived there late at night and was pretty tired. Needed some rest and sleep. We talked on the phone and the roads were wild and you were already in the midst of hardcore holiday partying, which I thought was good for you. After being in the desert for a while, I can only imagine how much your mind, heart, and body wanted to let loose. A sense of need for fresh air and freedom. No matter how wild and crazy it may be. I can relate. After global missions or disaster work, I feel the same.

Surprisingly, I crashed and slept well. If I had anything left to my sanity, it is perhaps due to my mind regulating me to sleep well.

I was awakened by your call and we decided to meet in Le Meridien, the hotel I was in, that morning. 25 December 2006. We met on Christmas day. Christmas gifts. I had brought some little gifts for you and other humanitarian workers. Just in case we actually met up.

So, yes. I walked down to the pool area, looked around, and there you were. Right across from the pool. With a head full of long black curly hair that was practically hiding your face. A tall, hardy, athletic Dutch-Indian man who looked like he just got out of the desert. We saw each other and pointed to each other, smiled, and then chuckled. Some situations are indeed surreal. I just had to laugh at myself at how Destiny controls most human encounters. The thought entered my mind. Now why did Fate want me to meet this man? Someone I need to know to lead me to my life's purpose? Ahhhh ... will just go with the flow. We hugged, we laughed, and you asked me to sit right there on the reclining chairs by the pool.

Before I knew it, we had stayed in those chairs, except for a restroom break, for more than ten hours straight. My God! Looking back, I think we must have gotten hypoglycemic and dehydrated.

What in the world did we talk about for ten hours? Almost non-stop. Very comfortable. Open. Honest. Straightforward. Listening. Talking. Conversing about life, our lives, love, families, friends, philosophies, missions, life purpose. A kindred spirit. Somewhere in those ten hours, I gave you a little gift. Merry Christmas to my comrade-in-arms. Colleague and co-mission worker. I gave you a book of O. Henry's short stories that contained "The Gift of the Magi." A beautiful story about giving, receiving, and love. You came over and sat facing me on my recliner. All the time we were talking, we were lying down on our individual recliners, or some-times sitting up, and we would face each other every so often. So then you kissed me gently. A thank you kiss. I did not move. Did not know how to respond. I also knew that you were a big flirt. You are much younger. I dated older men. Thought they were wiser. I also told you that you were taboo to me. But then again, our missions are most important for us, right? I was not sure what to think. Then I decided just to not think. Just enjoy the natural course of events. Keep it pure.

Finally you had to leave to be with a friend you met before I arrived there. I went on and changed to meet up with my other acquaintances. The French relief workers. We all were in the same plane together. Just in case I could not go to Oure Cassoni, I thought about joining them in the south of Chad to work with children. After I met you, I still did not know what to think. Jet lag. I did sense something. That we would be working together for our causes. That we would cultivate the deepest of friendships. And who knows?

Sweet Humanity

N'Djamena—29 November 2007

Such modern delights as a fluid Internet connection are not always available in Chad. In fact, where I will be working in the south it remains to be seen at what frequency I can respond. Every procedure, every act has its set pace. No way to speed it up. As I am not the world's most patient guy, this is a challenge. In fact, some people here whisper that I came to practice celibacy and to learn patience. Mmmm, we shall see. It comes back to utmost once again. To be self one has to drop all the veils of maya (the unreal world). Drop all habits that distract from the main goal here on the planet. To share the love with as many as possible. Distractions such as cigarettes, alcohol, drugs, gambling, gossip, violence, power, money, and women are all strewn in the path. I used to smoke like a chimney, but stopped at least ten years

ago (with some major relapses of hookah/sheesha). For now I am tobacco-free. Alcohol, the underestimated drug: It has been also about ten years since I regularly drank. I used to drink like a mad man. Six days a week. Last man standing. Massive quantities. All to be number one? Show off? Be stupid? Social practice of my peers? What is clear is that alcohol does not make me, or anyone else, I believe, a nicer and kinder person. It is for reasons of contemplative insight I have managed to turn my back on this vile drug. Other drugs have been a soma from the gods. Used in ferocious and copious quantities. For a long time. Somehow they give a false plateau feeling of all being well. A pseudo-utmost.

Yet all along I have always known that the best high is a drug-free high caused by a soul-searching deep conversation, an intense dance experience, the silence of friends, a meal prepared for loved ones with the utmost care, the singing of songs together or walking in the mountains. Gambling was and never has been my thing, nor gossiping or wishing others bad luck. Again violence reared its ugly head. Usually in combination with booze. Verbal aggression and vandalism. Luckily, almost never physical aggression. Some part of me has always seemed to be able to understand that violence is truly base. Well, anger issues, temper tantrums are part and parcel of my persona. Something that is hard to work on, yet I try. Meditation certainly has helped but I can still blow a fuse over small things. Power versus force. Books have been written about it. What I can say is that I believe every person on the planet can make a major impact if, and only if, he or she truly believes that walking the talk is required. A focused and dense goal will lead to success. Money is overrated. Yet it is essential in making the world go round. It is the expression of the value society may have for your specific skill sets and should therefore be happily accepted.

About women, I can write books. And Liz, it is where I have the most problems. On the one hand, women are like mothers, goddesses, wisdom, gentleness, strength in one. On the other hand, strife and conflict may come from not being with the right one. As you always say, celibacy is a great way to focus on work. And truly it is. It is just so hard to achieve. Most bad habits I can shake. I would never call women a bad habit per se, but womanizing is. What I wanted to say here is quite simple and straightforward. A combination of purity and mischief is the best path to the utmost. As it is called in the Bhagavad Gita; all issues related to the ego need to be dropped and the target is within. Self-control, self-application. For the bettering of humanity to one's fullest capacity. Feeling sad about past errors or present ones is not a productive route. What matters is being and growing, feeling the awareness inwardly that the human capacity to go beyond is nearly endless. Habits are just ego desires and can be released. Insight comes when the time is ripe, and words need not be spilt, but actions will show the pure path.

Dearest Liz,

Good things are happening in Chad and even if it feels like a standstill for now, I am quite sure that in a week's time I will be working like crazy. As I said, university teaching is the first thing that is materializing. Next the clinical work in a hospital, then consultancy for another NGO, and last the start-up of our NGO, Africa Vision. When patience develops, good things happen. I am off to sleep now and will write in response to our meeting in Chad this morning.

30 November, 2007

Dear Liz,

Is it possible to have a full-time job, write three books in a year, work on spiritual growth, go on relief missions, dance, giggle, plant trees, be a wonderful cook (?), care for family, friends, and anyone who needs it? Play guitar, harp, piano, flute, dance Flamenco, do Tai-chi, mentor talent fully to achieve the utmost? Mmmm … I know you do all of the above and more. Sheer endlessness is the positive energy when you are focused. As you often demonstrate, all it takes to write is inspiration, perspiration, and a keyboard. Hack away while making horrendous spelling mistakes. What matters in the end is that the ideas flow freely. I have told you often about my desire to write, and lately I find it easier and easier. It is clearly a vocation, but also a skill that one can develop by homing in. The reactions I am getting to my blog are pretty mind whacking. Inspiring people is always fun. And it brings me to the following.

If by written word so much can be achieved, imagine the impact of the spoken word, and an additional hug. The human capacity is endless! Sometimes it seems trapped under desires, wishes, ambitions. If you let go, all will be achieved. Not a funny pun or word game. A truth. *The Secret* has a note on it, I am sure. Comes another factor. In my belief, most of the capacity is already inside the body, heart, and mind. Just waiting to be unleashed. There are periods in life you are perhaps more prone to learn, but with a little bit of effort this period should be extended to the end. All is insight and insight is all.

Let the bookish knowledge remain in the books, participate therein, as in conversation with friends and colleagues. The truest and purest of insights will come when you are at the utmost rest and focused. In the zone, as sports people call it. When the needed three-pointer swooshes off your palms one second before the beeper goes. Or when in the hospital ten or more patients are asking for your immediate presence, and with a smile you trust the gut, triage to available nurses and colleagues, and all is like a flow.

The flow as I noticed, I maintained quite a while in the USA. It has to do with clear-cut goals and focusing on them to achieve and succeed. I am looking forward to coming back to the USA. This time, the goals will even be higher. National television, national radio, newspapers, an average of three talks a day at high schools, universities, human rights groups, church groups, or anyone that would lend me a soapbox. Awareness raising and networking are important, but this time I will add the component of fundraising.

Relaxation

30 November, 2007

Ashis dear,

Great to talk to you on the phone! No static. Clear. Happy to hear you feeling good about teaching. Lots to impart to others and the knowledge (baton needs to be passed on). You will excel in that. Mainly because you are an avid learner and thus will be a dedicated teacher. The teacher usually learns more as he teaches.

Wishing your mom a happy birthday by phone yesterday was fun. We were both on Skype at that moment. *Viva las comunicaciones.* Such a delightfully loving lady she is. You are very fortunate. We laughed so hard about my seemingly beyond-repair cooking skills. Imagine being in college doing your best to get a good grade in chemistry only to blow up three beakers in a row. Even when the teacher monitored what I was doing, the beaker

still blew up. That set the pace for my cooking complex. And believe me, it is not from lack of trying. I even read cookbooks. Isn't that utterly absurd? Considering I hardly cook, I am so appreciative and thankful to all the wonderful cooks in my life. In the Philippines, we had help cooking. When my kids were young, we had someone cooking for the whole family, and my ex-husband enjoyed cooking too.

My talent is in appreciating delicious cuisine. There is an art to cooking. And my grandmother said that food cooked with love is always the best. I shall not give up. My family told me that the man I truly love is the one I will cook for. Hmmmm … that is quite a challenge. My strategy is to go to a French cooking school, maybe at Le Cordon Bleu (I say that with an impish smile on my face), wherever, and learn. And your mom is kind enough and offered to teach me how to cook. And then I hope to cook a fantastic meal for family and close friends. My intention is to shock them. With love. And you already know me. An actualizer, much like you. We dream it and we manifest it. All in collaboration with the universe.

This is one of my first vacations in five years where I actually did not do a global mission or relief work. There is a strangeness to it. I don't exactly know what it is. Yet the rest and relaxation are doing me a lot of good. After my mom passed away last year, and then recently my brother, and my brother's father-in-law, it was good just to be there for family. And that allows me to pace myself, reflect, sleep late without schedule tensions, and just take it easy. However, my thoughts do meander off to Haiti. It would be great to meet Dr. Paul Farmer, who started a state-of-the-art clinic that helps the poorest of the poor in Haiti. From what I understand, he has gone to Rwanda to do the same thing. It would be inspiring to learn from what he does.

I was supposed to fly to Haiti this week. There will be another time soon. Embrace delays. Sweeter times to come for sure.

Right now I am also contemplating about Peru. I truly want to go. The earthquake devastated so many there. Lots of rubble and dust. The Hands On Disaster Response crew are working very hard. Their photographs reminded me a bit about doing a medical mission in the Zambales area of the Philippines. That was when Mt. Pinatubo erupted, leaving lahar, or volcanic ash, everywhere. A friend and high school classmate who is a cardiologist ended up with pneumonia, and so did I. Does giving my utmost require no rest? I think not. Resting is equipping our spirits to eventually serve more. Resting also combats secondary stress, compassion fatigue, and post-traumatic stress.

I recall how exhausted I felt after the Katrina hurricane relief mission in Houston, Texas. While vacationing in Oregon, I called the authorities in Houston to see if I could help.

Judge Eckles's office called me back to say yes. So I left the Baylor Emergency Room physician in charge my name and number to offer my services. Somehow, they got my name and followed through.

The number of people needing medical services within the Reliant Arena and convention center was staggering. Everyone there did their utmost in helping others out. However, it was clear that America was not quite used to disasters. Yet the evacuees were amazing. Though many lost their family members, or their relatives were displaced, incredibly, they did not lose faith during the devastation. In fact, their faith heightened. Moments of joy occurred whenever relief workers were able to put together lost family members with the rest of their family. There were stories about people traumatized by helplessly watching as their relatives were carried away by the waters while they were on their roofs. Some evacuees were traumatized by seeing dead people floating by while they were hanging on to something for their own dear lives. And people told about their utmost fears while watching the flood waters rise up so quickly all the way up to their heads and feeling so powerless and hopeless. Some talked about feeling doubly traumatized by the violence and rape that occurred in the New Orleans Dome. Those who were diagnosed with chemical dependency were suffering withdrawals and those who had mental illnesses did not have access to their medications. That created total mayhem.

I ended up with Bell's palsy. Perhaps the combination of acute disaster stress, a left ear infection, a harsh and very loud noise level, along with reduced defenses, led to that illness. I was on my way back to Louisville, Kentucky, and while on the plane, felt a numbing of the left side of my face. Suddenly I could not drink; the water dripped toward the left side of my chin.

I did a quick neurological exam on myself to make sure I was not having a stroke. Everything was fine, except for my left facial paralysis. That was an ordeal indeed. I could not close my left eye, my left ear felt steadfast, sharp throbbing pain, and my face became asymmetrical.

The good thing is that I discovered that I was not as vain as I thought I was. I had several scheduled activities where I was the speaker—churches, psychiatric meetings, and conferences, and I helped jump-start the first annual Talentfest for our non-profit mental health comprehensive care organization. Yup. I even ended up playing the electric guitar and singing a song I composed called "My Child." To be able to sing, from time to time I had to hold up the left side of my face. I truly don't know how I managed.

One of the things about having Bell's palsy was that I could not whistle, and worst of all I could not smile without my face appearing to be grimacing. I could handle not whistling, but not to be able to smile was heartbreaking for me. I love smiling. However, the Bell's palsy did serve me well when I did my conferences. It was as if God gave me that mask—that traumatized face—to share with others the pain and angst I absorbed from the evacuees who suffered. And who am I to feel sorry for myself? This Job-ian temptation can be gripping. Feeling sorry for ourselves can slip us into the detached and isolated world of self-centeredness. Some say that self-pity is the opposite of spirituality. Whereas the former derails us into a spiral inward into the abyss, the latter unites us with All.

The stories shared with me by the refugees helped me stay resilient. By knowing that they maintain their faith and their hopefulness, I learn to do the same. If they can handle it, that teaches me that I can too.

My brother Jun was very supportive. And I will not forget him feeling so much compassion about my Bell's palsy and saying to me, "Don't worry, A-te Liz. Now people will see your inner beauty more. I am really proud of you." My brother loved us all to his utmost. I miss him terribly.

Presently I am fine. I can feel some residual left eye drooping when I am tired or when my face gets whiffed with a gust of cool breeze or wind. You will not believe the joy I felt when I first became aware that I could smile symmetrically again. I will never take for granted a smile ever again. And I can even whistle a happy tune once more. I am grateful.

Flashback. Smiles. Remembering you taking off your clothes except for your yellow Speedo swimwear by the Hotel Meridien poolside. Yellow fever indeed! Since I was still jet-lagging some, things appeared to happen in slow-motion for me then. Then you went off and dove into the pool. Yes. You swam your enthusiastic butterfly strokes, Mr. Rainbow. Your IRC friends were all teasing you. I was not sure what to make of it. I just shook my head, went with the flow, and laughed. I had been going to the airport very early in the morning each day to check on my luggage. Dancing around the pool with another friend from UNHCR who had her iPod with her was lots of fun. The photographs taken were just hilarious. I could not believe it when you posted it on your Flickr. Mischief. You and me dancing our hearts out. Incorrigible. Comedic release to counteract all the sadness and fears all around us. Humor to the utmost. For our spirits' joy. Even in the midst of chaos.

1 December 2007

Wee hours of the morning.

Howie and I just came back from helping friends decorate their nine-foot-tall Christmas tree. It was the first Christmas tree Howie had ever decorated, so it was fun to watch him have a great time. He is doing his due diligence in preparing for his interview for the psychiatric residency. It was good for Howie and Tom to get to know one another. They are both like brothers to me. We had some beautiful Christmas guitar music while decorating the tree, and I took lots of photographs.

Remember when you and I went over to Tom's house and just hung out on his balcony and talked about our dreams, goals, desires, wild stories about what we went through during our residencies, until very late at night? Well, I took lots of sunset pictures right from that balcony overlooking the Ohio River. I mean, I have become a sunset paparazzi. Yes. Precisely why your mom calls me Little Miss Sunset now. And I call her Mom MoonGlow. And yes, you are Mr. Rainbow. Symbolic lovable terms of endearment. Each with their own familial meanings. So sweet.

I spent today preparing for my very first book signing tomorrow at Caffe Classico here in Louisville. My coffeetable book, *Your Compassionate Nature*, seems to be developing a life of its own. Family and friends have become enthusiastic publicists and resources. It never ceases to amaze me what friends can do to support one another.

Caffe Classico is also the hangout place of my other flamenco-dancing friends, and the ambiance is warm and lively. Very Latino. I feel at home there listening to people play the guitar, sing a la Gitano Flamenco, and dance my favorite dance. Flamenco. Flamenco dancing is such a beautifully externalizing dance that allows the depth of emotions and expressions with each stomping and hand movement. The passion. The *duende*. That spirit that takes over when one gets into the trance of dancing. And then the *genio* or temperament that makes profound the heart of the dance. The matador-like posture of a male Flamenco dancer and the confident, feminine, and passionately proud posture of the female dancer create a marvelous vision of the joy in *vive le difference*. The utmost dance for me.

Purpose

6 December 2007

I just read this quote by Eleanor Roosevelt: "The purpose of life is to live it. To taste the experience to the Utmost. To reach out eagerly without fear for newer and richer experiences."

Quotes like this, old wisdom, confirm a lot of what I reflect upon regarding giving my utmost. A book by Oswald Chambers entitled *My Utmost for His Highest* discussed the author's oblation and utmost dedication of his life to God in every way. To his utmost. For him, everything he does is for God. An incredible book of faith to its maximum. How do we give our utmost? Each moment? Each day?

7 December 2007

Look what I found here, Ashis. An old blog from last year, when you and I were talking about your concern that Chad might be forgotten by people. In dealing with the painful Darfur situation, it is important that people remember the many ramifications of its dilemma. How this Sudanese crisis becomes like an octopus that crawls out into the neighboring countries where the refugees seek shelter.

I remember writing this blog, wishing I could do more. If not for the constraints of my full-time work, I would have remained there for a while longer. I also wrote in this blog about my concern for you and your safety. And about seeing honor in what you do. The word "utmost" must have already been in my mind when I wrote this last year. Just read the last paragraph.

Liz's Blog Postings
10 December 2006

Remember CHAD
~ Compassion is Love's passion ~

The act of remembering is a precious tribute to the lives of the people we remember, delicately preserving them in our minds. An homage to those who have touched our lives in profound ways.

The people in Sudan are still suffering tremendously. The unimaginable genocide that is happening there has aroused the international community to make stands against the Sudanese government. Diplomacy and tough love from other countries presently seem to no avail, though. Dedicated humanitarian activists like Gabriel Stauring of StopGenocideNow.org recently made peaceful demonstrations against genocide. The chaos in Sudan is now insidiously seeping into CHAD and CAR (Central African Republic). The refugees and humanitarian workers in the camps are now even more vulnerable, as the rescue organizations are not able to provide adequate security. The situation is unfathomably dangerous, the risks inordinate.

Right now a colleague who works with the International Rescue Committee, and had worked with MSF, is in the midst of all this havoc in CHAD. As the last vehicles from UNHCR left the refugee camp in Oure Cassoni, I can only imagine how it must be for this spirited and honorable physician to take on the responsibility of health care for twenty-six thousand refugees. Each day, he lives with the uncertainties of potential violence toward him, the refugees, and the other humanitarian workers. His soul cries out to the world for us to remember CHAD. For us not to look away. For us not to abandon them. Here is Dr. Ashis Brahma's weblog: http://www.bahaibeach.blogspot.com.

My heart aches for him, for the refugees, and all the workers there who are now in a precarious predicament. For now, advocacy is most important. I promised him that I will spread the word to remember CHAD. To remember CHAD is to also remember Sudan, CAR, Indonesia, Philippines, Thailand, Sri Lanka, Uganda, and all the other places in this world with refugees and evacuees who suffer the devastation of manmade and natural disasters.

To remember CHAD is to remember those who have been traumatized, tortured, abandoned, oppressed. To remember CHAD is to remember those who are dying, who are ill, and who were killed. To remember CHAD is to remember the kindest depths of our souls, our ability to love with utmost compassion, and to remember the people who are one with us in spirit. To remember CHAD is to remember those who have been forgotten and can easily be forgotten if we turn a blind eye. I remember CHAD. Let us all make a stand. Spread the message. Remember CHAD.

posted by LIZ

http://garciagray.blogspot.com/2006/12/remember-chad.html

6:51 AM

2 Comments:

Ashis said …

Liz,

This region requires that we comprehend this fact: The time for talking is over. Smoldering chaos is now turning into mayhem … It will be even more intense than Rwanda if we do not take care … or if we forget to care … Be courageous. Care.

Liz said …

It was so good to meet you in N'Djamena, Chad, Ashis.

What more will it take for this bedlam to stop? Rest well. Stay well. Be well.

Keep that Tibetan crystal always close to your heart.

Namaskar,

~ Liz

Compassion Comfort

5:50 AM, Louisville, Kentucky

Utmost Compassion. If compassion is love's passion, then utmost compassion means giving the ultimate kindness and love to others, even if it's beyond what we think we humanly can do. With passion, it is as if a divine spirit takes over knowingly about the higher plan. Love and light come out to the world. The illumination of spirits toward oneness. How do we show our utmost compassion for others? Prayer and meditation? Asking the Divine for guidance and listening for that still voice to discern the will of God?

Every little act of goodness, is its utmost—in its own way.

Back to the present. So, now you are back in your element, Dr. Booffaloo. And you will need the Native American buffalo

medicine spirit in you. For strength, focus, and herding many to your cause. A stampede. ;)

Back in the field. There is nothing like it. Right there with your boots on. Serving many with your skills. Utmost purpose. To give of self the best you know how. I can relate deeply.

Though truthfully, the biggest temptation perhaps is complacency and comfort. Nothing more enticing than my soft cushiony cloud-like featherbed. In the relief work and medical missions, some of the beds are fairly comfortable yet some are truly restlessness-inducing. But nothing like one's own comfort zone. The very familiar. The little haven we have created on this earth. While in the midst of disaster work, besides my mental snapshots of tranquil nature and visualizing the faces of my family and loved ones, I also imagine the comforting feeling of sleeping in my own bed. However, my love for the missions is much more than my desire for what makes me feel comfortable. And that illusory comfort we have mind-created is nothing more than a dream. Temporal. Ephemeral. Maybe even unreal. Not something that sustains the life of the soul.

On the other hand, faithfully following a life purpose does maintain that zest for life and living to the utmost. At least for me. *La chispa.* The spark. What seems comfortable dissolves into oblivion, overshadowed by the even more heartwarming light of utmost service to others. For at the end of the day, and when I start looking back even just a little bit at my life, what makes me comfortable now is being right in the middle of missions and disaster work. My comfy-bed piece of heaven becomes merely a symbol, a reminder of the human need for balance between our work, play, and respite. Rest so I can work and play more. What

I hope to keep discovering and learning is how to make the most uncomfortable situations become comfortable.

Ashis, frankly, some things that were once very comfortable now feel uncomfortable to me. Yet my goal is to find peace and comfort in each moment, whether it is perceived as comfortable or uncomfortable by my psyche. The comfort in discomfort. The discomfort in comfort. Live each moment with love. And treat each moment, no matter what, as a parcel of infinite heaven on earth. Every moment a time zone of comfort. Anywhere becomes our haven. Hard bed, featherbed, or even no bed at all. Love each situation. Love each place. Love each utmost moment. No matter how tough and uncomfortable. Some may see this as pure wildness. Yet for now I am beginning to learn that each moment anywhere, and no matter what I do, is my little comfort-zone featherbed in disguise.

10 December 2007

Tranquility of the mind has come to me. Why, you ask? Because I am doing what I love to do. Different things with different people in different places. I liked what you said about the comfort zone. Even in N'Djamena it is so easy to slip slide away in a comfy life. Nightlife, dinner with friends, five-star hotel swimming pools. Nothing wrong with any of those, but it is the combination of relaxation and perspiration that makes the big wheels turn. Even if the area I am working now in southern Chad is less violent, it is still part of a country where a small minority rules with a hard hand over all the other minorities and the complete majority. Utmost nepotism in all its ugly forms. And yes, there is a relationship between the conflicts in Sudan, CAR, and Chad. And let us not forget the ugly role several countries like France, the USA, China, India, Russia, and the EU play in the conflict. The conflict is not singular. It is a mélange of oil, natural resources, dictatorship, neo-colonialism, corruption, the clash of new values versus old.

Liz, have you read Chinua Achebe's book *Things Fall Apart*?

It is an extraordinary story of Christianity overtaking the animistic way of life in a Nigerian village, with the added element of a "normal" military coup in Africa. It becomes even more sad when you realize that one year after the book was written, the coup did take place as described. The story was written fifty years ago, and it is still as valid as ever.

I'm looking forward to the classes I will be giving on public health. It is an honor and a pleasure teaching students of medicine in what I will call creative public health. Using common sense, and village wisdom, to identify the local priorities and to address the issues with a flexible mind—aiming for the highest impact at the lowest possible cost. I hope the students will be proactive and open to discussion. If not, that way of discourse needs to be opened to them.

With all my heart I hope that Africa Vision, our new non-governmental organization, will take off. It was the first reason I came to Chad. It's going to need nurturing and a bit of luck to get over the hardest hurdle—finding the first donor. This week I will give it a long, hard push again. And I will also try to find other sources of money.

What do you think, Liz? Is working without salary the ultimate freedom, or madness, or impossible, or all of the above? Do you feel like I do that money-wise everything will be all right? That good intentions will lead to a good outcome, even if not always the one you set out to achieve? Is a backup plan to join a big NGO again perhaps not a bad idea?

All I can say to all these questions right now is that sitting on the fence for a bit is good, but I desire to get into action, to establish a definite direction. As I said earlier, a mixture of perspiration and relaxation is required to make Ashis a well-rounded boy.

13 December 2007, Doba, Longone Oriental

So what is this drive to dip in to Africa's deep soil? Is it the music? The food? The people? The landscapes? The vibe?

A gazillion reasons could be mentioned, but the most important one is that life here is lived in its deepest sense. And what does that mean?

Distractions are to a minimum. Struggle for life is the main theme. It means that even while suffering there can be joy. The threshold is hunger. There are not that many children or adults capable of keeping a sense of humor with an empty, rumbling tummy. Nowhere but perhaps in India have I seen humankind's most beautiful feature, the smile, pop up so easily. The laugh for laughter's sake, banter, stories, enjoyment, dance. A friend once told me that my biggest gift was my playfulness. It is true. Wherever I go I am always clowning around. Learn a few silly words, do some dance moves, smile at people, talk nonsense.

Life is too beautiful to moan around, weighed down by the obstacles seen on the path. Africans get it. There is no need to argue. So when you do it, do it well. Fight, forgive, feel, share, be savage. Life is cheap and yet at the same time it is sacred. Take a look at the dowry. It takes a long time and a lot of collaboration in a family before a young man can raise the required number of cattle. Primitive? Nope, just different.

What is the utmost in civilization? Cultures where more than half of the marriages end in divorce? Where therefore a large number of children grow in a one-parent household, or with half brothers and sisters, stepfathers and stepmoms? Or where the woman has to endure the man having either a second, a third wife, or several mistresses?

Embrace the ambiguity! Between both ways, none is best. All are the human condition, just different expressions thereof.

Being of Indian and Dutch descent, I had an outsider's viewpoint from the beginning. Now I'm progressing to a deeper understanding. All are expressions of the same. Universal love. Call it divine or humanity or whatever you want, there is a layer of sameness in all cultures.

I just feel at home doing what I do, caring for the vulnerable in the place I find there is the most neglect.

True basic facilities as vaccinations, doctors, schools, roads, drinking water, and toilets are often not available where I work. Yet you will always find youth and older people passionate to improve the plight of the people in their village. I adore that commitment, that spirit. A willingness to step up. Altruism or not is not the issue. The issue is that out of a respect for life, a love for others and self, good things can happen.

Today two young nomadic kids were brought into the hospital. One was shot in the neck, one in the buttocks. Neither complained when their wounds were washed. They endured the cleaning with admirable strength. Because of their nomadic lifestyle, they are often described as dirty, simple, or primitive. The essence of what I saw was a loving and worried father, and his two boys who showed remarkable resilience and extraordinary strength even while in pain.

Look beyond the differences and ultimately you will see the same in all humans. After the Cold War a new common enemy had to be found. Such is the nature of mankind as well. Thriving apparently when there is a common enemy. A war on terrorism—and indirectly on Muslims—was declared.

I want to write about the religious dimensions of Chad where I am now, but will close my eyes to sleep for now. Tomorrow a twelve-hour drive to N'Djamena and it is getting late. Time to pack the bag.

Here in Bebedja there is time to reflect. Times stands still. And it is a good place to ponder on why I keep on searching for the road less traveled. Forcing a deep effort to accomplish things that could have been done easily in other settings. It has to do with balancing the edge, looking for the best in oneself and more.

For now, Liz, sleep well in your divine bed.

The Divine Spark

16 December 2007, N'Djamena

The inner child. The divine spark. It. Different names for the same. If you follow the path, meditate, and you can feel and hear the wisdom bubbling up. Self realization. Endless acceptance, and yet strive to improve, and beyond that strive to be. Let go of the material desires, emotional desires, all desire. Be, just be. This is the path for me; clearly a bumpy ride. There are many attachments to overcome. Yet the moments of wholeness, with It, the divine spark, the inner child, that I have reached (and hope to reach on a more regular basis) are what it is about. Utmost self.

Serve without wish for any compensation.

Give, without desire to take.

Take when it is needed.

Maybe it's a paradox, but the inner child will lead the way.

Whenever I felt most out of balance in my life, furthest away from my perceived ideals, acting out or acting without consideration, at some point the inner child gently nudged my heart: "This is not what you want to do, pal. Redirect the path you are taking; it is all in your own hands. Be the best you can be, and excel beyond. Lose the requirement for attention, find humility, servitude, honesty, and most of all, a sense of humor."

In humor lies many of the answers. The court jester was a dangerous power to be reckoned with. Beyond sarcasm, irony, and joke there often lies a shifting of perception. A different way to look at something that is common. Use humor as a tool to make yourself understand. Warp in and out of reality. Look from a frog-eye perspective and a helicopter view, and be part of the conversation at the same time you're an observer of yourself and others. Focus and you will see that all is possible. Not even the sky is the limit. Limitlessness is the limit. Utmost focus leading to utmost joy. Leading to utmost achievement.

Is there a need to accept less? Nope. The only way is further understanding of human nature in relationship to self, others, and environment. Deeper reflections, combined with inspiration and insight through meditation.

I do realize that a conceptual framework is needed, and study of the language and other modes of communication are needed to help us converse with others. To find the inspired conversation with self, where the golden laughter is never far away, is simply a matter of deep listening.

Listen, Ashis, listen.

Breathe in and out.

Hear the whisper.

All will be well.

The inner child, the divine spark, will lead the way toward what is your innermost desire: the desire to be desireless.

Today utmost is to be 100 percent self, to realize and accomplish what that self is wanting: realizing next steps. The unity of all life and the connection. For some this involves a form of God. For some it does not. For all, I hope, the consensus is that it involves a deep love for life, all life. An understanding of our intricate interrelationship.

I can hear my inner child giggling. Big words today on paper. Now just go out there and give someone a smile or a hug, or write a kind letter. Be your 100 percent best. Play, banter, laugh, be your youth and old age at the same time. Be in the moment always.

Love and Peace,

Ashis

21 December 2007

Yesterday was a most tender day. A memorial day for my brother, Jun. My sisters Lisa and MaryJo and my stepmom Barb (who, by the way, is Irish-Dutch), all met up at the Galt House. Ashis, do you remember the place where we ate, with the revolving restaurant on top, with the view of Louisville? In the lobby, many people were milling around waiting for the metro police shuttle, which then took us all to the Jefferson Memorial Park.

The Supporting Heroes organization is simply phenomenal. Utmost dedication for our fallen heroes and their surviving families. The executive director, Eric Johnson, is a retired police officer who has made it his mission to make sure that the families and survivors of firefighters, police officers, and EMS are remembered, valued, and supported.

Lisa and a member of another firefighter's family were in front, carrying a big wreath with a blazing red ribbon while the rest of us walked behind. We made a procession together to lay the wreath on a marble statue of a firefighter rescuing children. A symbol for healing our grieving souls. Honoring the honorable who gave their utmost sacrifice to the world, their own lives. Many of us could not contain our tears over the loss of the loving physical presence of our loved ones. I miss my brother Jun terribly.

Afterwards, we all went and had lunch at the Galt House. Meeting some of the surviving families provided so much consolation and support. People who profoundly understand the meaning of having to deal with the loss of those we loved so. The whole ceremony was beautiful. My family will always be grateful for all the kindness of those who cared enough to organize the ceremony.

Ashis, you wrote a lot of insights about life that made me smile.

Now we can acknowledge that our comfort zone truly is where it may be uncomfortable for many, and even for us. Embracing the ambiguity of feelings and thoughts.

And about the divine spark? We both have a lot of that, don't we? Our inner child keeps that utmost spark lit up, indeed. That inner being that opens us up to endless possibilities in life.

I want to have that awe and wonder about everything. That gentle innocence and delight in the moments, and the people who make one's soul giggle. That giggle can turn into bursts of laughter, once we realize that most of what seemed grave really had a lighthearted side after all. When people are finally able to laugh at themselves and at what they have been stressing about, that is an excellent indicator of their being on the road to health and healing. And sometimes giggles happen just because of sheer joy. Spontaneous. Rays of joy that generate smiles all around.

About your dilemma over balancing how long you need to keep donating your time and finances to your projects—the uncertainties, the absence of any guarantees of what the outcome will be—I believe you already know the answer to that. That is certainly something between you and your Source. Listen, Ashis. The inner-soul whispers. Listen deeply with much love in your heart. What do you truly hear? Perhaps the answer lies in there. Just my thoughts. They also apply to me.

You know what you have to do. The mission. The riveting edge. I also know what I have to do. A blend of nobility, madness, naiveté, and deliberate dedication to a worthy cause. The belief that all will not only be well, it will also shine. The utmost Light.

Some thoughts. After the memorial for fallen heroes, I went back to work to see my patients. Holidays are difficult for many of my patients, but more so for those who lost so many loved ones because of Katrina. One bright admirable lady with much inner strength lost family and friends in New Orleans. But even after she started renewing her life, one devastation after the other came along to darken her life even more. Relentless, merciless destiny. It has ranged from losing her husband to another, to an accidental fire in her home, to suffering depression, to her children suffering the effects of ongoing tragedies, to going through painful physical illnesses. How much more can she tolerate? Yet she does. She goes on. She is back in school to be a nurse. Amazing, enduring spirit.

People can be in heaven and/or hell wherever we are depending on circumstances. How do we cope and deal with tragedies? Some cope with much anxiety and some cope with grace. And there are those who use their tragedies to give hope and compassion to the world. The ones I called "Phoenix Miracles" in my other books. Role models for coping with life.

27 December 2007, Back in Louisville from New York City

I pondered about quite a few things while in New York City the past few days. There was something magical about witnessing a young couple dreamily dancing in the midst of the Grand Central Station. Perhaps that sight just spoke to the hopeless romantic in me. The couple reminded me of watching my grandparents dancing to Johann Strauss's waltz, Tales from the Vienna Woods. Imagine walking into the house and seeing them dancing, realizing how much their eyes were only for one another. The parents of ten children, and so many grandchildren too, and still being in love like that. The couple in Grand Central Station replayed my grandparents in my mind. My heart smiled seeing them. A beautiful Christmas gift.

And after that was a mind-boggling kaleidoscopic light show, holographic projections of Christmas-essence images and goodwill for everyone twirling all around the walls of Grand Central Station. Music. Applause from the traveling crowd, which certainly must have had people from all over the world, for this surprising holiday entertainment.

I started taking digital photos of the station, inside and out. All kinds of angles and compositions. While I clicked away, a sensation of inner peace gently caressed my heart. Jacqueline Kennedy Onassis came to mind, and I suddenly realized the value of her artistic vision for this magnificent historical building. Utmost artistry. Structural elegance. And most of all, it was the melting pot for blending together all the diverse travelers from around the world.

I could hear so many languages spoken by various people in the crowded station. I felt a sense of familiarity run through my soul.

At some point, a man who probably suffered from chronic schizophrenia started to shout out loudly to people, proselytizing irritably about Jesus and the need to be saved, yet I still felt that serenity. Perhaps I got tranquility from momentarily knowing within that this crowd was a symbolic representation of all the people in our world. All walks of life. All cultures and creeds. All One.

I sat on the stairs with other people who were watching all the happenings in the station, only to notice that there was a sign warning people not to sit on the stairs. Well, several of them probably did not even speak English, so the sign meant nothing to them. Maybe my Eurasian features hinted that I might not be able to read it either.

Ashis, my most profound memory in this past NY visit is still that young couple wantonly dancing in the midst of a milieu, without a care in the world about what anyone might say. Just like my grandparents. A grand love. Maybe that's one of the reasons why I love dancing so much.

The subway trains were not jam-packed as I anticipated. The

holidays seemed to mellow many of the passengers. Many were on their cell phones, talking loudly with their loved ones. I had to laugh when I saw some teens nodding away to the tune of their iPod music, while close by there was an elder, a silver-haired lady, also nodding away to her music. That tickled my spirit. In my mind, I started nodding to the rhythms too, joining them spiritually.

My iPhone. Amazing toy. Imagine carrying around something that can instantly connect us to many parts of the world.

The train rides were peaceful and meditative. I took catnaps. Then I had good visits with my son. I admire his courage to face life and his inner self. I am grateful to be his mom.

The bursts of drizzling rain created a backdrop for serious contemplation about life and love. Walking around East Forty-second Street, where the New York Helmsley Hotel and Grand Central Station are located, was conducive to acquiring insights about the past year.

What came to mind? Bits and pieces of the two of us walking all around New York City. Blazing trails everywhere with our version of the Free Hugs campaign. Remember that? We were radiating love and hugs, everywhere and anywhere. That started in the MOMA. While we were sitting in the museum and just talking to various friendly people, the Free Hugs campaign—Ashis and Liz version—was born. We talked to the people we met, got to know them a little, and then provided them with random hugs. The best antidote to wars. More love and hugs.

Initially, folks did not know how to take us. That was understandable. I'm not sure that we knew how to take ourselves either. Yet there we were. Playing yet loving. Loving every minute of play. And much laughter. We giggled like two kids, finding humor in just about anything. There was no one who was a stranger to us—two happy physicians doing the Free Hugs campaign in New York City.

And the concept is heartwarming. I believe it is time for the medical profession to go back to the human-healing, inner aspect of medicine. And most of all, back to the healing power of the human touch, the human connection. So much can be given, and received, in a simple loving hug. We physicians have lost that to some extent. As a profession, we have become so scientifically minded, and so defensive about potential legal problems, that we have lessened the most valuable aspect of being a physician. Healing. With compassion. And with mindfulness in giving appropriate hugs, like our old family doctors did when they made home visits to their patients. A touch of the hand. A warm pat on the shoulder. A compassionate hug when someone is told about the severity of their illness. Or when there is a loss in their home.

But prior to that, Ashis, I distinctly recall my own concerns about you being accidentally detained, just because of your long hair, and your exuberance, and how much your appearance suggested someone stepping right out of the pages of the Bible. I wondered how security authorities might react.

It was clear that you were needing decompression after coming out of the Oure Cassoni refugee camp. You looked like a wild buffalo soldier, ready to stampede the place all by himself. And New York City at that. Coming from the camps, it was good for you to enjoy the finest accommodations as well. And why not the best? You worked hard. Frontline. And it was time to play and replenish. So, Waldorf-Astoria. We met at the lobby.

You looked ready to take on the world by its tail. I almost didn't recognize you. Laughter. Warmest hugs. Time to fill our stomachs with some Thai or Chinese food. We were loaded with stories to tell each other. Sometimes talking at the same time, sometimes listening at the same time. Yet not once forgetting the Darfur situation, nor the clean-water-for-the-world causes. Nor the plight of the vulnerable and the marginalized. Subtly, underneath all the laughter and joy, our hearts cried for the people who suffer from torture and contaminated water in Africa. And for those in situations that require the world's attention, those with AIDS or malaria, the incarcerated, the impoverished and the hungry. Can the world not see? Are we doing enough?

Nonstop conversations about everything while eating supper in a Japanese-Chinese restaurant where we ended up. We'd found a Thai restaurant before that, but there was a long wait. And our tummies were grumbling.

After that terrific meal, we both wanted to dance our hearts out. I mean dance until we dropped. It occurred to me that as much as I love dancing, I am glad that I was not in the rave generation or I could truly be in bad shape by now.

The flow. Follow the flow. That led us to a little dance place in Greenwich Village. We were not sure exactly where we were. Inside, there were bold, red, exotically patterned Middle Eastern-type curtains. Most of all, dance music filling the room with sensuous energy. And we danced. And danced. And danced some more.

With every dance move, it was as if we were shaking off all our angst, all our patients' sufferings and pain, all the world's problems, deflecting all those things away from ourselves. As if all the cares of the world were spinning away from us, flung in all directions by every movement of hip and arm. A physical, emotional, and spiritual catharsis through the freeing movement of our bodies. Almost convulsive, yet undeniably synchronized dancing. Freestyle. Inner and outer freedom. The rhythmic drumbeats reminded me of being with the Clean Water for the World team when we were welcomed with dances and music in Uganda by the Mubende community. Big grins and smiles on our faces. Resonating laughter while dancing.

After a while we were the only ones dancing on the dance floor. Until my feet started feeling some pain. New shoes. And then you were the only one dancing happily out there. I lay down in our red-curtained booth to elevate my feet and to rest. Every now and then you would do a little dance performance for me. And I would undulate and make comical dance gestures without getting up from the bench. Dancing to our utmost. I'm so glad to have those photos. Live, love, and laugh.

28 December 2007, N'Djamena, Chad

Dear Liz,

I can still feel the flow. Canton, Ohio. *The Betty Mac Show.* The way the two of us veered between seriousness and mischief. Your telling me that because we'd gone and danced in the fountain that morning, your hair was all flat. A beauty tip to be recommended to anyone about to be interviewed on television. The crowns we got from Burger King, and the look on the face of Mr. Eye, our photographer friend, when he saw us tumble out of the elevator crowned as king and queen. The beautiful weather; sun radiating from a light blue sky. The interview where flowers were handed out, and our going from a very playful discussion on the meaning of hugs to the plight of the people in Darfur. The need for grass-roots clean water programs around the world, and our role therein. The golden-voiced Justine telling stories about wanting to do projects in Haiti. It all came together. A feeling of belonging. A deep love for Canton, as a metaphor representing a deep love for all. Zooming in to the level of understanding that comes from joy and play, which then leads to the naked being.

Over the last year you have stimulated me to do what I love. Which is to write, then go out there and inspire, but also reflect and take rest.

"Homo ludens." Let us play. From play comes understanding. From play comes acceptance. From play comes universal love.

Shades of darkness have troubled my mind for many years. Slowly, however, an understanding percolates into my brain and heart—there is no need for that darkness. There is just some feeling, maybe a frustration, because experiences lived in Africa and Asia do not translate all too easily to lives in Europe and the USA.

Yet the human experience is one, and on the basic level all the suffering and joy that is encountered here in the continent of Africa can be transmitted: suffering and joy, just as in the Western world. The tours I made in the USA showed me that people really are touched by what they learn. That they do care. That they do want to make a difference.

I have talked a lot about dance for Darfur, or Scrabble for Sudan, or Candlelight Dinner for Chad. There can be enjoyment in fundraising and awareness raising. With a smile and a laugh you reach the heart more easily, and it is from there that a change will come. A nonacceptance of the brainiac view that the status quo, the grand divide between the materially rich and materially poor, should forever stay intact. My experience shows, Liz, that the largest numbers of smiles, and the deepest felt, are found in areas of spiritual richness and material suffering. There is not a bone in my body that does not wish economical development for developing nations, yet to my mind the key remains in happiness for what is available. Loving and caring for others or humor come freely when the basics of peace, health, shelter, and food are there.

30 December 2007

Dear Ashis,

Right now I am listening to the radio and listening and singing along to Richard Marx's song "Now and Forever" as I write. Naturally, I find it more appropriate to change some of the lyrics to fit a woman singing it instead. Multitasking indeed. Here I am actually really just resting for a change. That leaves me a lot of time to contemplate about life and love. And as I pause, thoughts of us walking around Times Square find their way into my consciousness. The lights. Bright, ubiquitous neon signs. Your mom has told me that the last time you visited New York was when you were only four years old.

The air was so crisp when we were in that city together. Lots of people everywhere. We were just walking around wherever life led us. Sweet, easy, joyful times. Suddenly we came across a group of Chinese artists drawing sketches of people's faces right there on the sidewalk. And so why not? There was something about the street lighting that night. The artist immediately went to work on sketching your face, using charcoal. Sitting down right next to the artist, positioning myself so I could actually see what he was seeing, was truly an eye-opener for me.

You may disagree, but I still think those photos I took of you really got your essence. And the sketch of your face definitely needed to be sent to your mom as a gift. The sketch resembled you very closely. The artist was able to capture your features well, though he had to work hard to get a true likeness, especially of your unique and multicultural nose.

There must have been something in the streetlight's whitish glow that night. Maybe the spirit of joy radiated everywhere from just our anticipating the sheer mischief and fun we would have all around the Big Apple. Playtime. It was good to see you with such a nonstop grin, as big as Africa, after you'd come out of the desert of Chad. While I watched the artist sketching your essence, unexpectedly and momentarily I saw that light of your being. A special moment of perception.

I just did not know what to make of it. You looked very happy and calm, yet so connected. For me, that seemed enough at that time. My heart smiled an utmost smile in the midst of knowing that it was enough to care about someone's well-being and happiness. The photographs showed your dreamy-eyed face and a sense of inner peace. Yes, that was good enough.

Back to now. Benazir Bhutto, Pakistan's former prime minister and their country's champion for democracy, was just assassinated in the town of Rawalpindi three days ago. I communicated with a humanitarian friend from Pakistan. He told me that there were some isolated riots in Rawalpindi, but that most of the mayhem was in Karachi, where Bhutto had lots of supporters. Sad times for many in Pakistan and the rest of the world. Even though I'm an apolitical person, it still saddens me when political leaders are killed because of their beliefs. Her death reminds me of the time so long ago when John Fitzgerald Kennedy was shot while waving to an adoring and cheering crowd in Houston, Texas. Will we truly ever know exactly what happened to him that day, to all these world figures?

My mind floats back and free-associates in Times Square. I'm thinking about taking photographs, and when the huge neon sign in the background saying the word "Virgin" made me laugh. Hand in hand, like two children just out of school, we walked and skipped around the most visited place in Manhattan, talking to people and spreading some love and hugs around.

My memories are coming in bits and pieces now, kind of shuffled in their chronology. They are starting to appear like sepia vignettes, with light touches of primary colors on the objects around us. I still have lingering thoughts of walking around Central Park, getting lost in what seemed to be a beautiful maze.

We continued our Free Hugs campaign everywhere we went, and we met interesting people from all walks of life. Remember the two elderly ladies? One had an especially beautiful and memorable face, and seemed very articulate and distinguished. As we did our hugs, we went right telling people about our causes, clean water for the world and Darfur refugees.

Then we set off toward the Dakota, the apartment building on Central Park West, where John Lennon lived, because I am such a devoted Beatles fan. We got all turned around and started to duck under trees, climb over rocks, and steer ourselves through bushes, trying to find a reasonable pathway. In a clearing, we met a Gypsy-looking lady with a radiant face, and also her African-

American partner. She was selling some arts and crafts and had woven bracelets and handcrafted jewelry, wearing a long, funky, psychedelically colorful hat. Her entire outfit made her look like she came out of the '60s.

After we talked to her about our Free Hugs campaign and our missions, she looked intently and compassionately at both of us and said she wanted to give each of us a present. She asked me to raise my left arm and she selected an intertwined yarn bracelet of golden yellow and white. The gold was "a symbol of joy," the white was for "pure love." Then she asked you to raise your left arm, and she wrapped the green and white yarn bracelet on you. The dark green represented integrity and the white was again for pure love. Time somewhat stood still. She blessed us and wished us the best in our lives. After that, we quietly walked towards the park fountains. That whole encounter was like a trance experience. We, the loudly excited, unstoppable rabble-rousers actually became silent, absorbing the moment.

Then I started to tell you stories of what our little group of friends called Hearts Coming Together, who want to change the world and make a difference, did in the Bellevedere fountains. You know them all. Some of our Omidyar.Net friends. The group all splashed around in the Belvedere fountains and had a great time while talking to people about loving life and discussing what we could do for the homeless. That was in April of 2007. We were still feeling mellowed out by our experience with the Gypsy. There was something soulful about our chance meeting with her. I'm not absolutely sure what it was, but it felt lovely.

On your Skype call today, you sounded tentative. God gave you another chance in life once again, Dr. Buffalo. You told me how you had been attacked, and robbed, by a couple of men who were probably drugged out. You fought them, but from past experience you knew that they were more interested in the few material things you carried. Probably to buy more drugs and alcohol. They took your money and passport. Thank goodness you were left unscathed. Perhaps all the prayers of family and friends who love you cloaked you with an aura of safety.

I am so happy that you are alive and well, Ashis. We both have more to do. You also said that you had a premonition prior to the incident, a thought that you ought to have taken a cab. It was no consolation when you finally told me that one of the men had a knife. That brings back memories of last year, when you and your Oure Cassoni refugee camp bodyguards were assaulted. And when your driver got shot. You initially made light of it, trying to allay the fears and anxieties of loved ones. Most probably I would have done the same thing just to calm down my family and close friends.

Yet what is it that makes both of us do what we do? Going right to the frontlines of potential danger to serve others? Do we just have some latent suicidality that we exhibit in exposing ourselves to potential harm?

After much serious contemplation, I think not. Because we unquestionably both love life to our utmost, and with all our hearts and souls. Which is probably why we both feel compelled to serve the most vulnerable, so they can have at least have a fighting chance with life. A life you and I treasure and have been enjoying to the maximum so far.

Though you are now in the south of Sudan, away from the Chad-Sudanese border, the imminent dangers in Chad have regrettably heightened. Especially for humanitarians after the L'Arche de Zoe French aid group incident. Members of Zoe's Ark have recently been convicted and accused of kidnapping 103 children in an unauthorized airlift, reportedly with the intent of exploiting the children for adoption in France. The Africans were understandably outraged. According to the news, the children were mostly Chadians rather than Sudanese and the majority were not orphans.

The Zoe's Ark relief workers contended that they were trying to take the children from harm's way. Some local Chadians were implicated. Clearly, there needs to be a lot of repair of trust before the Chadians can regain a sense of comfort with, and respect for, the many humanitarian relief workers needed in their country. All of these events naturally affect you and other nongovernmental organizations (NGOs) in securing funding for causes. The deeds of a few can often imbalance the good intentions of so many more.

Heartbeat is the restaurant you proudly discovered in the midst of NYC. You wore your handsome, light grayish-blue suit and tie. I wore my black off-one-shoulder asymmetrical pantsuit. Dressed to dance. We cleaned up pretty well, didn't we? We were laughing about all the time I spend dressed in scrubs, and you in desert fatigues, during mission and relief work. So this time, it almost felt like we were going to the prom. My lacy, sparkling, silvery shawl came in handy for the night. And of course, you made sure that you had your special hair conditioner, made with olive oil. Heaven forbid if we didn't have that.

The conditioner indeed made a sweet difference. Photos prove it. The restaurant was conducive to privacy. Warm ambiance. Excellent, friendly, and solicitous waiters. Great food. Our conversation grew softer, and we could not stop smiling. That was just before we went out dancing in Greenwich Village.

More sparks of memory are coming to me. We meditated in Central Park. Well, sort of. We found a wooden bench facing a grassy lawn. The sun was gentle on our faces and that warmth felt sublime. We were silent, soaking in the rays while being in a meditative mind-frame. My mind went blank. Only to be awakened by the low, breezy sound of your deep breathing. Your head kept bobbing, and sometimes would land on my shoulder, and mine must have been doing the same thing because it felt like I was in and out of twilight. Maybe we both actually fell asleep. You resolutely maintained that you were meditating. Okay. Sure. I just had to smile. Whether we meditated or fell into a power nap, we enjoyed some gentle, easy moments of bliss.

What Is Most Important?

1 January 2008

Happy New Year.

My dear Ashis,

May the New Year bring us all inner peace, hope and much love. My mind is still filled with tender memories of our Skype chat the other day. Like a delayed reaction on my part. Hindsight can be so brilliant. In many instances, going through a life-threatening situation opens up a period of reflection about our life path. Layers of existential angst and questions can suddenly engulf us. Where are we really going in this life? What do we really want? More to the point, what do we truly need for our own spiritual growth? What are the life lessons being learned? And we look at our relationships and start wondering about what is most important. The meaning of love. Who do we love? Why do we love? We then start looking back to our past as well as ponder upon our present. Who are the people around us whom we love and value most? And why?

We wonder if we should settle for less or aim for our utmost, even in our relationships. And what does it mean to experience our utmost in a relationship? Then we start weighing things. Who are the ones we can't live without? The ones with whom we have soul connections so deep and strong that life is difficult to envision without them.

When I did disaster relief work in Thailand for families affected by the tsunami, there was one night in which several of us thought we would die. Another tsunami warning was suddenly broadcast for Khao-lak, right where we were, the area that had already been hit by a big tsunami. People knocked on our hotel doors screaming, "Tsunami in twenty minutes." Everyone dashed uphill for safety. All of us thought that it would be over for us in a short time. My life truly did flash before my eyes.

The most important, most meaningful people and times in my life ran through my mind with such speed, yet somehow combined with surprising slow-motion gentleness and inner peace. I wrote about this experience in my other book, *The Courage to Encourage*. When we are forced to realize that our time is actually limited, and that physical life will not go on and on, something clicks within us to make us want to value the precious moments and people in our lives to the utmost.

Once we actually survive scenarios like that, where life could have just gone like the wisp of the wind, we profoundly reflect upon life and love. Have we said all we needed to say to the people

we care about most? Have we left anything unsaid to people because we were on the fence about something, or afraid to express
our true feelings? Perhaps you may have gone through some of
that. After surviving the second tsunami warning in Thailand, all
I could think about was wanting to hug my kids and all the family
and friends I love, and simply be with them.

I was touched by the things you said to me just the other day.
Normally, we say things with much humor and we tend to play
with our words and our conversations. However, the tête-à-tête
and heart-to-heart context and tone of the dialogue are vital. The
melody between the words and beyond the words has more sig-
nificant emotional value. This time you were more serious. At one
point, I thought I may have misheard you. But then you repeated
your words in such a serious manner, it made me pause. Part of
me did not want to hear it because I know what may happen.
What I already knew inside. And what I have been resisting and
wanting to deny all along. For many valid and important reasons.
That gradual opening up of the heart. For I did not even fully
know what it all means.

I tried to alleviate my minor anxiety with some wicked humor. I asked you if you said what you said because you were in a
weak moment, realizing that you recently could have been killed.
You came back with a quick-witted answer, that you felt the same
way "even in stronger moments." For now, I will just let go and let
God. We are powerless over many of these things. When Destiny
unfolds its course, the road is paved toward its destination.

Crossroads

2 January 2008

Dear Ashis,

Crossroads. My past splashed over me yesterday. Just when I have been deliberately working on being a tabula rasa, having a clean slate from people from the past and past experiences, I surprisingly received a couple of heartfelt, profound poems. What to make of it? Not quite sure. The poems made me pause. They were moving. However, I need to keep moving forward to where I believe God wants me to be. God's will, not my will. I need to go where there is love and where I can serve and give my utmost love. Please be still, my heart. Life and Love will go where it needs to. And we are right inside its train.

Thought about you today, Dr. Buffalo. I know you are also going through some soul-searching about your life and about someone you were trying your best with. I sense your disappointments about things at times. Life will put us where we need to be. And not necessarily where we want to be. Perhaps when we learn to start wanting what we need for our spiritual growth, that is when we truly feel our bliss. Wishing you the best always.

Hugs and love,
Dr. Gazelle

3 January 2008

Dearest Liz,

Yesterday I received the greatest news.

My brother and his girlfriend are going to have their second child and they are moving back to the Netherlands in four to five months. One of the ways to embrace life is to be part of that rejuvenating and refreshing experience of parenting. It must be such a blessing to be presented with a divine miracle, a brand new baby. The utmost expression of love. As you have said, "love's wish to perpetuate itself." I am delighted for them. I told them that this is by far the best news of 2008, and will remain that.

At the same time another path has been popping up in my mind. Love humanity with all your heart. Let all children be part of your love. Not mutually exclusive, these two paths, but accessible to those with the freedom to roam in time, place, and person. A family does give added responsibilities.

What I am trying to say here, Dr. Gazelle, is that no path is better or worse. Each gets its own deal in life. Your own karma. I may be blessed in many ways, and kids may not be on the path. This past year has been a year of immense growth. Taking time to meditate every day for one hour. Shelling out free hugs to all takers. Random acts of kindness, daily appreciations, all have led to a much more positive outlook on life.

And then there is the Dr. Gazelle I met. An *amiga* to laugh with, to write with, to dance with, to eat with. Everywhere we go turns into a little kindergarten. A place where we get the maximum of love out of the people around us. The club in New York with the hookahs, where we danced until the floor trembled; the restaurant in Louisville with its revolving floor. The utmost for me has to do with the childlike quality you possess. To wonder, to enjoy, to have limited inhibitions, to be fearless, to be in awe for life and loving to live, always wondering how to maximize the pleasure in an innocent way.

You have made me realize that what I want is what is within grasp. Becoming a writer; just do it.

Becoming a public speaker; be one.

Becoming an advocate for refugees; throw your heart out.

Becoming a better person; be loving and follow the golden rule. Do not do to another what you do not want to be done to yourself.

In reflection over the last year, these are all places where I can make progress. Setting the highest standards does not mean a lot; it is about the path toward finding that inner beauty, the inner calm, the inner child. For Hindus this can be called Krishna consciousness. There is the realization that God is part and parcel of you and of all life surrounding you. Different religions have different names, but to me it is essentially all the same. There is a divine inspiration within all of us. Everyone has their own view on this, and a right to their view, and that fact should be accepted. My view is just one, and who am I to blow against the wind?

Dearest Dr. Gazelle,

It has been a remarkable year. I am in a bit of a lull now. But I am sure it is only seemingly. I am focusing on my creative energy. In an attempt to unload the soul and mind, I try to get as much writing done as is possible every day. Then there is the teaching of medical students—so much fun to prepare the lessons, even if the facilities here are bare minimum. It just tickles the mind to be creative in ways to challenge those limitations. I will be talking to them about public health. "Creative public health," as I wish it to be seen. Using common sense and inquisitiveness to come to maximal health benefits for the people of Chad. While the government is doing its utmost to remain in power through following a path that is the opposite of love. A path of destruction. A path of war and exclusion. A path of self-aggrandizement, at the expense of all.

One should have a look at the hospitals and health care centers to understand the plight of the average Chadian. Diseases like malaria and diarrhea are abundant, and are major killers. People contract vaccine-preventable disease such as measles and polio because the distribution system has broken down, or because at a central level the vaccines have been sold for profit. If I remember correctly, it was just last year that Transparency International ranked Chad ranked number one on the list of most corrupt nations.

There are no quick-fix solutions here: the current government can only be ousted by a coup. After which you can wonder if the country will be better off. At least this evil is a known evil. Within this setting lies the challenge to keep on working for the benefit of the lesser privileged.

Does all this mayhem of civil war, discrimination, deception, and manipulation make Chad a hopeless case?

No way!

There are no people who deserve the label hopeless. What is required here is the insight into the human capacity to endure, to suffer, to be resilient, and most of all to be joyful despite it all. No need to turn a blind eye to all the suffering, yet at the same time there is no need to wallow in sorrow.

Chad will eventually become a democracy. Only a decade ago there were few real democracies in Africa, but right now the examples are plentiful. Africa as a whole has been having a greater economic growth, on the average, than the rest of the world. If this century will be the century of Asia, let the next one be the century of Africa. It takes a while for a continent to get swinging, and Africa has all kinds of potential to become the queen of the prom.

Dr. Gazelle,

Our talks indeed are usually full of play. But after going through a robbery you get an overview of what is worth what in life. The way the two guys went about their attack was almost slapstick, and my first instinct was to fight. I lashed out and bashed some noses, until I saw a knife and instantly realized I was doing the worst possible thing. By then I had only to win by handing over my phone and money. Who wants to talk about those little things when there is your life to worry about? This was not the first robbery I've ever experienced. Looking back, despite all previous exposure and training, my initial reaction still seems surprising to me. Most important however is to be able to make the right decision after a string of bad ones, and not look back.

These guys who robbed me are known to the police and will end up in jail eventually. No need to feel angry about them. They just do not know another job and are into the habit of alcohol and other drug abuse.

I needed a warning, apparently, that my sense of security was skewed to an unreal level of confidence. That warning I got. And I have taken my measures.

Liz, I am going now to prepare my classes. For public health I'm using kala-azar, the parasitic disease, as an example. Next time I hope to be able to talk about refugee health. And it will be in French, yippie ay ee.

All the best and a brilliant 2008 with a plethora of books.

Love,

Dr. Boofaloo

Dance

4 January 2008

My dear Big Boofaloo,

The new year has made me realize what a great buddy and soul partner you have been in this past year. And mission playmate. I thank God for you, Ashis. Right now I remember the look on your face on the day when the city of Louisville gave you all those awards: a key to our city, a declaration of Dr. Ashis Brahma Day, and an honorary citizenship of Louisville, Kentucky, for your humanitarian work in Chad when you were with the International Rescue Committee.

Well-deserved. And I am proud of you. Everything you learned in Medicins Sans Frontiere, IRC, and all your other training prepared you for last year. But what could have prepared you for dancing in the Canton fountains right in the midst of the city,

in broad daylight? How liberating was that? And how symbolically cleansing. Wishing that everyone in the world had that kind
of clean water. And contemplating, while dancing and watching
the abundant, refreshing water all over us, about all those in the
world who are still dying from contaminated water.

It does not make sense. We have a lot to do. We meditated and
prayed sporadically while playing around and dancing through the
fountain with those two graceful ladies from a local dance troupe.
The music was polyrhythmic, dance inspiring, again reminding
me of the early sunrise drumbeats of Africa that make me want to
dance until I become oblivious of time and space.

And then we went to Betty Mac's television show with my
frizzed-out hair. Betty is truly an incredible talk show host. So
articulate, warm, and personable. There was great heart chemistry
among the three of us. Bursts of laughter on the surface of each
question and answer.

Thank you for having driven me to Terre Haute, Indiana,
when my brother Jun passed away. You were right there in the
midst of my family while we were grieving so hard. And you
helped console us all by just being there quietly.

Of course the drive there was another example of a comedy
scene popping up in the midst of a tragedy. At least it was every
time that I drove. I admit, my driving is not the best.

You actually are quite a safe driver and that was helpful. We
conversed about everything, as always. It was so comforting to
have you there. Have I thanked you yet for that? Seeing my sister-
in-law Elisa cry and feel the depth of her grief was more than I
could bear. Elisa and Jun were so in love, and their love was like a
light for us all. Then we had those moments of irreverent laughter when I introduced you to my dad. I said that many think

you look like Jesus. And dad quickly responded, "Well, maybe he is."

I remember us dancing in the Fourth Street Live in Louisville until we dropped, celebrating the success of your talk about Darfur and the awards you were given. We were trying to find my colleagues and friends at the cathedral, but we lost them somehow. And remember when some ladies came right up to you, one of them laughing and the other in a blackout drunken stupor, hallucinating that you actually were Jesus Christ? Then they turned to me and they called me Mary. And so I said, "Okay, are you referring to Magdalene or the Virgin?"

I just have to shake my head and smile when I think about how many people we were able to talk with, laugh with, dance with, smile with, and hug with. Spreading joy and laughter everywhere. The man-child in you uplifts the woman-child in me. We may be prime examples of Robert Fulghum's message in *All I Really Need to Know I Learned in Kindergarten*. Not being childish, but being as a child. Childlike, with pure-heartedness. Innocence. Honesty. Playfulness. Loving.

And speaking of children, many of the kids I work with have been abused in every way possible. A few years ago, when an extraordinary teenage girl started talking about her life, it was hard to hold back my tears. Her own father prostituted her for drugs. From the age of eight she was mercilessly raped, and physically and sexually abused by older men. Drugs and alcohol compounded the chaos in her life, and she had been in and out of detention centers, rehabs, and hospitals.

The way she expressed herself as she talked about her unfair and agonizing past, the depth of pain and suffering in her soul, her almost beaten-up spirit, the quiet tears that streaked down her face, well, that got to me. After so many years of being a psychiatrist, there is no desensitization to feeling empathy for a child or a teen in their agony. Somehow, this amazingly spirited adolescent was doing everything possible to someday recover and reclaim her spirit and her life. And then one day, at a very young age, she rock-bottomed. And from there, she had nowhere else to go but up. She detoxed, was put on some mood stabilizers, learned to pray and to meditate, and was adopted by a loving guardian.

Years later, there she was in my office again. This time she was beaming and beautiful, all dressed up professionally, so proud of now being a social worker who championed abused children's causes. We hugged and we could not stop smiling. She gave me thanks for helping her and being there for her when she felt she was at her worst. I thanked her for teaching me about the human spirit and love. We both were able to laugh about the past in a way to say goodbye to it.

She has become who she is from what she learned about her experiences. There have been many more stories similar to this one. And also stories of other teens who we lost to relapse, even though our staff worked so hard with them and cared about them. Their memory still haunts us.

Children have the right to live their lives with joy, love, and compassion. As you know, even with the best love we give our kids, or despite the worst abuse that may happen to children, Fate has a way of dictating what truly happens to our children. There is always a bigger picture that we can never really decipher. So we just learn to love them all we can, for all the moments we are with them.

By the way, congratulations to your brother, his girlfriend, and your newborn nephew, Yannick. Your parents must be quite happy. And I know that you are glad to be an uncle again. All kids are our kids, Ashis. I think that you are discovering that more and more. You know that you and I would take a bullet for any kid. And you are just like that big buffalo in the Youtube.com video who rescued a baby buffalo from the lions and crocodiles.

I posted the following on DailyAppreciations.org today:

~ I appreciate reviewing and opening the door to the past, just a little bit, yet not dwelling on it. Mainly to learn from it. To smile when we discover that the past teaches us and equips us for the present. And that the present is a soulful playground for a future that will only lead us to evolve and realize that we are love.

~ I appreciate crossroads. They lead us to choose which path to take from many choices. Only to discover that all paths are paths to Love. And we take the path where we are led most by deep love for God and others.

Freedom

5 January 2008

Dear Ashis,

Great to hear your voice, Dr. Rainbow. I want to add something to our talk: Life has a way of putting things in our laps when we are still and not even reaching for them. We talked about the feeling of freedom. It is all relative. Remember when my brother-in-law, David, told you that he felt his freedom most being with my sister. And Marissa will be the first to tell you that she is very clear and structured with David. Within the perceived structure of their faithful love for each other lies his sense of freedom.

For me, spirituality holds the foundations of utmost freedom. No matter what, freedom is there for me when there is deep love. For the love expands our hearts to be so all-encompassing that there is no sense of emotional, psychological, or even spiritual incarceration.

Freeing myself from past attachments is like cleaning the slate. The proverbial virgin mode. A mind and heart free from distractions.

And that is a heart free to be open once again since I got back my key. It is amazing how any of us can be temporarily locked down in our souls without realizing it. Dragging on irrational old feelings in our hearts that don't need to be there anymore. Mostly because of feelings of hurts or disappointments. And so we unknowingly and accidentally close our hearts to those who give us much love, even those we could potentially love more than we love Life itself. I would rather go on with my life alone than settle for anything or anyone other than the utmost. And the utmost to me has always been Love. I believe in it.

For now, I shall be still. Fate is the driver and seems to have its own direction. So many things have been showered on me all at the same time, within just a couple of restful weeks recently. Gifts of opportunities and expansion to extend the reach of missions are overflowing right now. Networks of humanitarian connections are there wanting to support our missions. A silent, clear, and focused mind is necessary to discern what needs to be done. To stay balanced and centered is necessary. Most of all, I need to keep my eye on the mission. And allow this tornado of brewing opportunities to twirl around without disturbing my own inner peace, life purpose, and sense of love and joy.

You seem to be in a similar mode. Wanting some things to work out, but feeling unsure about some circumstances. Going back to India will be good for you again. To reflect upon your life and how it is going. What you have been learning and, most of all, the wisdom you are discerning. And yes. Because you are an avid student, I can also see you eventually as a guru. Any student who is dedicated, spiritually open to learn all, is building the best foundation for being an exceptional teacher.

Most importantly, I believe that whatever life brings us will be for the best. And when we learn to believe that every second we breathe is an utmost experience of love, then our lives will flow in a way that will astound us even more. When we hold that belief, it means we have learned that the depth of gratitude and appreciation in our hearts is the key to our joy.

5 January, 2008

Excerpts from an e-mail letter I sent you today. My free associations:

Right now, there is a feeling of freedom in my heart. Perhaps the new year brought it on.

Lots of writing and reflections. Finally letting go of something emotionally that has needed to happen for at least a year. My soul feels more peace.

I think I just did not know how to love anyone enough to want to work anything through. And that's why I stayed in limbo.

I think for now it is best for me to just enjoy feeling free, and at the same time stay mindful that I should not be so wide open that I am unable to focus on the spiritual work at hand.

I never gave anyone else a chance in the last few years. My focus was close to unshakable. And a lot was done.

Frankly, I like purity in a relationship. And the kind of purity I am looking for in a relationship does not have much to do with sex. Yet I want to be clear that I think sex and making love can be very pure between two people who love one another deeply. Seeing the humanity *and* the divine in a relationship are both vital.

I am referring to the purity of mutual honesty, mutual respect, and mutual love. An ability to want to uplift what is best for the other's well-being as primary. Nothing absolute nor perfect yet close. I need a semblance of that to remain focused on the missions.

Destiny is capricious. It creates twists and turns, and then zigzags even more. We need to discern what it wants us to do. And perhaps things just happen. The path of true love is never smooth, according to Shakespeare. And Gibran said it well about Love: "But if in your fear you seek only Love's peace and Love's pleasure, then it is better for you to cover your nakedness and pass out of Love's threshing floor, into the seasonless world where you shall laugh but not all your laughter, and you shall weep but not all of your tears."

There is a big secret part of me that just wants to stay in my home office and not have to deal with all that is falling in my lap right now. Yet there is a lot of light and love in the flow. A whole lot. And that illumination needs to be shared with the world.

Fate. Kismet. That path may be the most jagged of all, yet it's a path worth taking if the world will benefit from the utmost brilliance of light and love.

Memories

Dear Ashis,

My mind is reliving memories of my last few hours in Chad. I'm not sure why. I went to the airport early. After I had checked in and my luggage had passed through security, I ended up waiting for my flight in a little room just off the main lobby. The only person there was an elderly lady selling Chadian arts and crafts that she had spread out on a small mat on the floor. Perhaps she was hoping that people would want last-minute souvenirs for family and friends. The rolled-up canvases were paintings of women doing chores and I bought a couple of paintings of Chadian women bearing water jugs.

We two were conversing, just talking pleasantries in Arabic, when the electricity suddenly went out. We were far from any window, so there wasn't a single ray of light. I closed my eyes in order to stay in my center. The lady grabbed my arm, and I grabbed hers for support. She started praying out loud and I was praying quietly too. I tried opening my eyes again, trying to make out shapes in the dark. Nothing. Then things got very quiet for a moment, followed by what sounded like shots outside. Probably Kalashnikov. We did not know. She gripped my hand much tighter, and I could sense her fear rising. I just kept whispering to her that it would be okay. And I felt comforted by hearing those words, almost as if they had not actually come from me.

I remembered how, when I was preparing for this trip, I read reports about the takeover that happened at the same airport in April of last year. Great! I wished then that I hadn't done the reading before this mission. Then we heard whispers, low voices, and someone, apparently a security guard, asking us in French if we were okay. I answered "*Oui, merci.*" The lady asked what was going on. The security man said softly that he didn't know yet, but that we should stay right where we were and he would let us know as soon as he could. She and I held hands. We felt a little more at ease, perhaps accepting that if anything happened to us, we at least had each other there. And if indeed it was another takeover, and we were to accidentally get shot in the process, at least we would have died praying. It's always amazing what goes on in your mind when you think that you might die.

Shortly after that, the lights came back on. We could hear people talking louder, some even laughing nervously. Big sighs of relief. People asking "What happened?" Then, it was business as usual.

I gave the grandmotherly lady a hug and we smiled at each other. Chances are I will never see her again, but I know that I will never forget her. For those brief moments, in that intense situation, it felt like we've known each other forever. Two perfect strangers had relied on each other's support, brought spiritually close because of circumstance.

After that, I saw our UNHCR friends who had been at the outer part of the airport when the blackout started. I was so glad to see them. Sadly, however, one relief worker seemed shell-shocked. She had strange, startled responses when anyone spoke to her. A wild look flashed in her eyes, and she seemed not just guarded but downright paranoid. The other workers asked me what might be wrong with her. I thought that she was showing symptoms of some kind of acute or post-traumatic stress. I sat next to her and just made benign and gentle small talk, so she would not feel reactive or stressed. Sometimes when people reach the edge, these defenses are how their minds protect them from the memories of the trauma. All I could be sure of was that she must have gone through some kind of deep pain, and I felt compassion for her.

Some more memories in Chad. One thing that I'd enjoyed doing there was trying the Seeing Beyond Sight experiences we learned about on Omidyar.Net through Tony Deifell, who wrote an inspiring book about this exercise of taking photographs while blindfolded.

Remember that sunset when I asked you to describe the colors while you were blindfolded? You were right on the mark, or at least very close, to describing them just as they appeared to my eyes. It was also spooky when you knew, without sight, that Dr. Ponce was then coming close to us.

Since I am always on a photographic quest for sunrise and sunsets, I practiced tai chi in the morning there in Chad, by the pool, when no one was around. I decided to try a double challenge—to see whether I could frame a close-to-symmetrical photograph with my eyes closed, right after doing a tai chi move.

Ahhhh, I know—the things I do to challenge myself in every-thing. I don't know why I do that. It's my own personal game. I just locked my elbows straight and clicked away. I also did that while we were driving around—had my sunglasses on and locked my arms and just kept on taking photographs. Interesting results. Some of them had such symmetry that you could not tell they'd been taken with my eyes closed. One of those photographs looks almost haunting: a boy was looking right at the camera when I clicked the shutter.

That photo was taken while driving around N'Djamena. Of course, there were photographs that were completely lopsided, but I was very pleased with the ones that came out with some symmetry.

It's amazing what "seeing beyond sight" does. All the other senses are heightened when one of the senses is deprived. In the Philippines, for instance, many people who suffer blindness are given jobs as masseuses or masseurs because of the awareness that their sense of touch will develop utmost sensitivity. Seeing beyond sight was also especially appealing to me because it gave me a little sense of understanding the conditions of my nephews, Josh and Jacob. They suffer partial blindness, deafness, and ataxia from an unknown neurological ailment. I also tried the experiment from my hotel balcony, overlooking the river and lush plants and trees that surround the hotel. The sunset from up there was quite spe-cial.

When I got back home alive and well from Chad, a part of me wanted to kneel down and kiss the ground. Meanwhile, an-other part wished that I was still there in the midst of missions. I thought I could have gone to the South of Chad with that French volunteer group. Later on, though, I was chatting with someone

who worked in the American Embassy, and he told me that return-
ing home had been a wise decision. Because of the international
political issues, it would have been difficult for them to assure my
safety. It was during the time of Saddam Hussein's execution, as
well as a time of transition for the leadership in the United Nations. Since I was not affiliated with any umbrella organization to
umbrella me in my relief work, my safety might be tenuous.

The trip from N'djamena to Amsterdam, and from there to
Detroit to Louisville, went quite smoothly. My baggage needed
six days to catch up with me, though. On the plane I smiled to
myself, thinking about the time we spent getting to know some
of your IRC staff. And I felt sorry for the reclining chairs at the
Hotel Meridien. I wonder if the ten-hour indentations we left on
them by our lazing bodies ever leveled out. I left Chad wishing I
could have done more. Somehow, I knew I would be going back
to Africa again. Africa has grown inside of me. I have absorbed so
many parts of its magnificently enchanting spirit.

8 January 2008

Dear Mr. Blowfish,

I was just thinking of the late afternoon when I had to drive
you to the Native American sweat lodge ceremony in Southern
Indiana. I was ultra-focused on my driving. I knew that the ceremony would be extremely hot, so I was wanting to make sure
that you would be well hydrated. So I as I drove along I kept in-
sisting that you drink the bottles of water I was handing you. And

I guess I spoke with such conviction that you obediently drank two large bottles of water back to back. Probably just to appease my apprehension that the heat in the sweat lodge might turn you into a gargantuan prune. Then you became uncharacteristically silent, so I turned and looked at you. Holy smokes! You looked like you were getting nauseous, and your face seemed to be swelling up. But the expression on your face was far too precious, in a strange sort of way, and feeling somewhere between concerned and startled I said, "Oh my God! You're starting to look like a blowfish. What's going on?"

And you said, "Liz, I already drank two liters of water before you gave me two more!" And we both burst out laughing until our stomachs ached. The kind of situation that only the best of friends can laugh about irreverently. You were like a human water tank loaded beyond capacity, but it was clear that you were all right. That was when "Mr. Blowfish" was born. That name just stuck every time we remembered what happened. And of course, Mr. Blowfish does have a counterpart. For my driving style, which tends to make people want to kiss the ground when they realize that they've survived another trip, I was graciously dubbed Miss Road Runner. Blowfish and Road Runner—partners in crime.

The gentlemen in the sweat lodge were friendly and kind. They seemed to be a laid-back crew. They had a hammock, so I decided to rest there and read a book. I heard all of you in the lodge praying. And then I heard you men sing Kumbaya, and I almost had to laugh. Even the white dog's ears perked up. Then all of a sudden I saw a hand stick out of the sweat lodge. I wondered whether one of you guys had just passed away, until the hand started shaking, and then it went back in. Of course, I learned later that it was your hand.

A little later you all started coming out of the lodge and just looking for a place on the grassy ground where you could lay flat against the Earth. Then each one of you spent some time alone, in silence. Each finding their own space. I did not dare utter a word.

Afterwards, we shared a meal and the other men talked about all the other sweats they had done. It had become night by then, and while we talked about everything under the sky, we also gazed at the stars, trying to name any that we recognized. The North Star.

You said that you felt great!

On our way back to Louisville we talked about the Native Americans. I was planning to go and visit the Pine Ridge Indian reservation in South Dakota. Pine Ridge is an Oglala Sioux reservation, and many people say it is among the poorest, if not absolutely the poorest reservation in the USA. My daughter Jacqueline has already done some volunteer mission work in the neighboring reservation, called Rosebud. I am very proud of her for doing that and for her loving humanitarian heart. My sister Marissa has already been sending donations to Pine Ridge, especially during the winter, when many of the elderly die from the cold. In the back of my mind—or perhaps in the forefront—I know that I will be going there.

The Native Americans have always fascinated me: their cultures, their lore, their tribes, all so rich in tradition and pride. I recall seeing a television commercial long ago, about a Native American man canoeing through a lake that was polluted. When the camera zoomed in close on his face, a huge tear was streaming down one cheek, as if to say, "What have people done to our Mother Earth?" That image always got to me.

Utmost

My wish is that when you come back here next time, we could go to Pine Ridge and see what we can do to serve. Most likely we shall learn a whole lot for our spiritual growth.

Love,

Da Ms. RoadRunner

Crazy?

Dr. Buffalo,

Crazy? In our quest for giving our utmost daily? Of course!

Many people would say that we are just plain out of our minds. Out there exposing ourselves to all kinds of circumstances. Yet a lot of what we do can be deemed as also quite balanced and sane.

Which parts can we feel proud of? Our desire to spread love and joy wherever we go. Our dedication to our missions and causes. Our love for our higher power and people.

How crazy can we be? Maybe we can be seen as crazy and sane all at the same time. Yet as Dr. Seuss wisely wrote: "Be who you are and say what you feel; because those who mind don't matter, and those who matter don't mind."

If the path to love and compassion is crazy then I must be crazy indeed. In my job, I have seen much wisdom that comes from the people I care for. We have to destigmatize those who suffer mental illness. Here in the USA, statistics tell us that one person out of five suffers some type of mental health problems. I dare say that there are way more than that, who haven't been counted because they have not gotten help. And the unwarranted stigma around mental illness keeps them in the dark, afraid to admit the truth to themselves or to others.

So, you and I may sometimes think that we are crazy. And perhaps other people may think we are. Love them anyway. Love us anyway. How insane is giving our utmost to the world? But I believe that the sanest parts of us may well arise from our efforts to do good in this world.

Utmost.

Giving

Dear Dr. Gazelle,

It was not a busy day at the hospital, yet those few that showed up did not fare well at all. The first kid I saw was a two-year-old. I put my stethoscope to listen to the heartbeat. It was silent. No breathing sounds either, and no reflexes when I shined light into the pupils. In other settings these signs would prompt us to try reanimation, but here it is not done. We have no ventilator, Ambu bag, oxygen, heart pulse meter; even dopamine and dobutamine are missing.

And there is more to these stories. A second child who came today illustrates best the cultural practice in this area. We saw an eight-year-old boy with cerebral malaria, and it was clearly going to be a tough battle for the child. We prescribed our medications, plunged in an IV line, and arranged the best possible care. He was unconscious and already showing signs of aspiration of the lungs, so we strictly advised the father not to give his boy anything to drink. Three hours later a nurse found the mother of the child holding an empty cup while she closed his mouth. Here it is believed that you need to have a last sip of water when you die, to help you on your journey.

What does it mean? The first kid was sick for a month before they came to the hospital. That might be because of a lack of funds, or a lack of understanding. But, sadly, sometimes the hospital is also a place where the death of a child is legitimized. Even if it involves one of the parents suffocating that child. The second child had not suffered a lengthy illness time, but he wasn't brought in until he was in a preterminal stage, and then he was pushed over the edge.

How to care for and be with people who can be so harsh to their kids? The answer is never easy or straightforward. In a way, when the children arrive here anyone can understand they will not make it. Then again, children are remarkable rebounders and can survive nearly any onslaught. Parents here love their kids, just as anywhere else. Somehow there is a threshold where their utmost love turns into a perceived final solution. A final rest for the child that is ill. Be it to protect the meager funds of the family, be it because there is genuine belief that the life of the child is over.

It is hard to fathom the utmost despair a parent must feel to take the life of his or her cherished one. I wish I could say these events are isolated, but nearly all patients present to the hospital in a dire status. It is rare to find an illness in an early stage. It is a way of coping with health that is common here: wait and see. The basis of the neglect leading to the final neglect is staged here.

Giving

When a perceived threat to the life of a child seems imminent, measures are to be taken to assure final rites of passage.

For the present, this is something for us to accept. Entering a dialogue, as is often tried, does not seem to change matters a lot.

Another main event of the day reminded me of my own former days of heavy drinking. If it were not so pathetic, it would almost seem funny. One sixteen-year-old had been out drinking with two buddies since midnight. At six the following evening, he decided to take a bike and ride home. His two friends were too inebriated; he was the one who stepped on the pedals and sat on the saddle. After going three hundred meters he crashed heavily on the road, nearly gouging out his eye. He was too intoxicated for surgery, so it had to be postponed. We had a battle on our hands even to clean the wound because he had the impression that he was dying and going to paradise. He spat all over the place and fought as if it were indeed his final moment. Finally we managed to cover his eye in a bandage. Then we locked him in a private room with two relatives. We placed him on a mat on the floor so he could not fall off his bed, as he was prone to do with his agitation, risking even more trauma to his already shaky head. Apparently this youngster has developed a habit of binge drinking. It remains to be seen what he remembers of his wild afternoon.

We have often discussed the alcohol-induced void. The moment that anything can happen because your mind is so wasted that the difference between good or bad actions cannot be discerned. As I've told you, I used to drink so much that at times I had no clue what the hoot I was doing. One of the best things I have done over the last ten years is to kick the habit. It is a way of utmost destruction. Double dangerous, as alcohol is a socially accepted and encouraged poison. As I still go out very often, I have plenty of chances to see what alcohol does to the mind and personality of people in the short-, middle- and long-term. It destroys the inner beauty, just as most drugs do. But this one is a definite ripper.

The beauty of feeling the need to self-destruct, or at least partially self-hurt, is the opportunity to realize that the opposite offers so much more. Self-destruction and self-love or self-realization are so far apart from each other that they go beyond being mirror images. They do not even exist on the same spiritual plane. I have gone through the extremes. Because I was feeling so little, I thought I needed to see the edge and beyond in order to feel alive. At least I thought so for a long time. But I finally learned that there is nothing boring in being tranquil, in a state of balance. In fact it is the utmost blissful state.

Dearest Liz,

I am enjoying writing. It is becoming a habit and it is even better to do so with a like-minded soul. Your fifteen-pages-plus contribution was full of insights and wisdom, stories, and anecdotes, a deep flow of thoughts and feelings. Just as it is when we are together. Like witnessing a big play. You have seen the video of our playtime in Canton. I cannot wait to see it as well. Perhaps we should add some clips to the book to make it a true multimedia event. I can say that dancing in the fountain was a blast, but it comes nowhere near to how I feel describing to another person the experience of being at rest, at balance, in a flow, enjoying joy, laughter, connection, and more all at the same time.

Belonging, utmost acceptance, is something you can search for but will hardly find. It is something that is unleashed, and almost never when you most want it or expect it. When it arrives, it comes hard and fast. All in our own way we seek to be accepted for who we are, including the nagging parts, or the insecurities, the downright bad habits and character traits, because together with the illuminated part it forms the whole of what and who you are.

Tomorrow I will trail blaze through pages 1–115 and see where our flow is going. As you said: a mixture of present, anecdotes, wisdom, mischief, banter, and play, but most of all showing an intertwining route of two like-hearted souls who want to give their utmost to make this place a better one. The daily appreciations, the random acts of kindness, the Free Hugs campaign, the Darfur awareness, the clean water campaign, the daily psychiatric patients, the daily teaching, the daily hospital patients, the sweat lodges, the meditation, and the dancing. They all lead to a better understanding of self and the interrelationship between that self and the bigger world around us.

So why even bother about the utmost? I'll make an attempt to an answer.

As I left for Chad this time, I packed one of my favorite books in a modern form, a DVD. And guess what, Liz? It does not work. My Baghavad Gita is not available to read. But let me tell you a bit about the book. It is called the nectar of Hindu religion and is the story of Arjuna, a fierce warrior who, just at the moment he is about to engage in warfare against his cousin and brothers, starts to doubt the motives of the war. His charioteer is Krishna, a reincarnation of the god Vishnu. Of the trinity of God he is the one that keeps the entire universe in balance.

Krishna does not mince words with the doubt of Arjuna. When you are born, your path is laid out. It is for you to act upon your duty. Destiny is laid out. It is up to you do your duty in life without pride or shame. Just do it! Wailing over the death of your relatives will bring you nothing. Are not all humans born mortal, and is the spirit ever not immortal? Why doubt the illuminated path?

There are many ways to interpret the story. Some say it is about the struggle between good and evil. For others it is the struggle within to see the Divine that is part and parcel of self. For yet others it gives clear guidelines about how to handle situations in life. Do upon others what you want to happen to yourself. Give your utmost—not out of self-interest but because you are part of the greater whole.

Today I was talking with the sister of Bebedja about the different nongovernmental organizations that have come through this region over the years. It is amazing to hear the same story over and over again in different countries and in different periods, created by different organizations. It seems that it is easier to give people a fish than it is to teach people how to make a fishing rod and fish for themselves.

The example she gave was easy to understand and unfortunately not uncommon. It is a form of self-fulfilling prophesy. During the war in the South a well known but not-to-be-named-here international emergency organization came to help out the local hospital with war surgery. All services were offered for free, salaries for all health staff skyrocketed, health staff was poached all over the country, a level of care was set that was beyond what was available in the capital N'Djamena. When the crises began to seem stabilized, the NGO pulled out. Destroying with its departure the existing health care system, which was based on cost recovery, with all patients paying a small fee to make the system self-supporting.

Is it the utmost good to deliver excellent, but unaffordable and unsustainable health care, undercutting the existing health care structures, and then to abandon the hospital once the sexy crisis is over? When you give the fish until the person forgets how to catch their own fish, you create a long-term nightmare.

We talked about the term *caritas*, to give, charity, to give without expecting that the receiver takes responsibility. To me this is a mindset that should have been abolished long ago. Nothing that comes for free is sustainable. If it is unsustainable, it has nothing to do with really caring about the uplifting of a culture, a region or a country.

Utmost would be to me to focus on knowledge transfer—even in a time of crisis—working with the means that are available on-site, in-country, without creating false illusions about non-available care once the White Land Cruisers have left.

Is a crisis intervention, then, not at all useful? Well, I honestly wonder. Development and crisis intervention are two hands of the same body, and should work with true coordination. Then people will have a continuum of health services.

Too often there is little communication between the two hands. That fact comes back again and again this year. Without funds it is hard to work. Big organizations have funding aplenty. But the work I wish to do is be a trainer of future fishermen. Giving the skill set and confidence, so that intervention from abroad will be minimal and rare, not a recurring event.

That's why I've decided to teach public health to the sixth year of the medical faculty at the local university. And also to work in a hospital in the deep south of Chad. I'll write about it, first in a blog and then a book, and I'll tour the USA to tell people about the potential of Chad and Sudan. Never give in, never give up. Talk about the good things that happen. That eternal human potential to excel, to shine, to laugh, to be.

Encourage people to open their hearts, minds, and souls for their kindred souls out there. Do random acts of kindness. Care about their direct environment and the bigger picture. Show the relationship that all living beings on this planet have. Make it clear why a conflict in Sudan is of utmost importance to someone living in Canton, Ohio. We are all one. Whatever affects someone in Bebedja has a meaningful relationship with the people of Louisville.

How can there be a desire for peace in the world if it does not involve an attempt to eradicate ignorance, the root cause of all evil?

Let us work on getting that message out!

It is so much more fun to love and be positive. Not to be blind to the negative things happening in the world, but instead in a state of mind capable of reframing that into positiveness. Too much time and effort gets wasted by being framed in fear and manipulation. We are taught to fear the unknown; I ask to embrace it. Unknown is a temporary something. Go out there and learn about our brothers and sisters around the planet. See the joy that goes around. Those having little to nothing can show all of us the universal joy that is part and parcel of human nature. Looking for that purity will lead eventually to the utmost bliss.

The two-year-old during morning rounds looked at me for

a long time. A strange face, unknown, but not unloved. As he showed by reaching out to grab my hand and take my stethoscope. He almost managed to slip it into his mother's bag. I'm hopeful that one day this young boy will be in my public health class in Chad.

If funding for my project fails I can always come back to Chad for a month a year to teach modules of public health to the young and coming doctors. Hoping to inspire them not to abandon their country and keep on working despite the strong appeal from foreign countries. Setting up networks with Western doctors, giving the Chadian doctors a feeling that they are part of the larger family of physicians in the world. And that working in Chad is not only hard but also lovable work. A job with a future in a country with a future. After all, even Mozambique and Angola came to peace after seemingly eternal civil war. Peace is just as much a part of the human condition as war is, and at one point good will overcome the evil, just as Krishna spelled out.

I see the Utmost whenever I see enjoyment in discovery. All children are born with this talent. And then our educational system and our elders manage to quench the fire. Questions are deemed difficult to answer, and eventually kids stop asking. Yet it is the inner child in all of us that gives ultimate joy.

There are always people wondering why I am so playful, why I want to know just about anything. Well, I had the good fortune to have parents who nurtured me in such a way that I could discover on my own pace—sometimes slow, sometimes rapid—what life is about.

Today, the eleventh of January, I am sitting in the emergency room of the hospital in Bebedja. The stream of patients has dwindled for a moment, and I've closed the door to dance to some

Bombay Beats until the next patient pops up. Balance the edge. Have fun. When working, work hard. When playing, play even harder. The morning round of our thirty patients in pediatrics and thirty patients in the medicine ward went fast. A few questions about patients who have been here a while, and some about new patients. Overall most are doing well.

I've just come back from the operation theater. One of our new arrivals has not been able to keep down any food and liquids for more than a week now. Her abdomen feels like a hard board. We'll need to do a surgical exploration. And the story, before her coming to the hospital, is as that story always is. She was sick at home for three weeks, not able to keep down food and liquids. Today the moment came when her husband decided that it was time to go the hospital.

Here, due to lack of education, patients nearly always come in at the late stages of their disease. Often too late. It takes a good deal of reflection to accept how this behavior often leads to untimely death. But that is how it is here.

Another lady is crying her heart out for all to hear. She is having her bandages replaced. She collapsed into a fire after a convulsion, burning at least 40 percent of her body. What pain and what endurance! The last lady who occupied the same bed was burnt even more, and after five horrid weeks she finally gave in. Her parents took her home to die in peace.

From the extremes of pain to the extremes of joy in a matter of minutes. Two healthy babies born in the hospital this morning. We oscillate between pain and pleasure, sorrow and joy, suffering and play. All in the same day. At times in the same person. Someone arrives in a coma after falling into a well; they leave a week later without any health problem. Or the opposite outcome for what seems to be a straightforward delivery, and the patient eventually leaves without the baby and without her uterus, because of complications that leave the surgeon no choice but to carve it out.

It saves a life, but it also leads to a life of suffering. In Africa a woman without a child is considered to be bad luck. A woman who cannot deliver is not a full woman and may be discarded by her husband in favor of a younger one who can deliver. Life shells out misery to some.

Dearest Ashis,

You addressed many profound ideas about why we seek to give our Utmost. And my mind gently overflows with thoughts about Giving. ChicagoNonProfit.org's founder Randy Dill has asked me to be the keynote speaker at an event for philanthropists and donors, and to talk about "the Art of Giving" and volunteerism. It will be a mixer where the philanthropists and donors can meet with the NPOs' founders and staff, and also with investors, realtors, and community leaders. What a brilliant idea.

Most of the time, donors do not meet the people behind the charities and organizations they want to support. There is nothing like face-to-face human contact, even in the age of the Internet.

Contemplating the reason for giving is akin to focusing on our life purpose. There are so many ways to give. The more creative the giving, the better. And it is so much more fun. We always receive by our giving. And do we ever receive tons of spiritedness from those who suffer the most, just by seeing them rise back up like Phoenix Miracles!

A simple smile. A warm pat on the back. A reassuring nod. A listening ear. A tender look. Making and giving time for people. Giving compassion, kindness, undivided attention. Empowering others. Encouraging others to soar and fly. There are so many nonmaterial things that we can all give one another. Sometimes, the thing given may well be some tough love. Most of tough love is tough on the giver. It is much more difficult to be seen as the ogre than to be deemed a sweetie-pie.

This is especially true in interventions with loved ones who suffer from chemical dependency and/or mental illness. To really help others, a certain firmness is necessary during interventions. Most of the time, we prefer to give tender, gentle, compassionate love. That always feels easier. However, many times, helping others requires doing the tough thing.

Material donations of effort, skills, and funds are also vitally appreciated. Many times, donations are given pragmatically, for tax deduction purposes. Sometimes, people donate because of guilt after seeing reports of the tragedies on television. Images of all the starving, emaciated, neglected children often compel people to donate. But very soon, perhaps after one flurry of guilt-based giving, people begin to just look away from the photographs of traumatized, suffering, and dying children. This is one reason why it's a good idea to encourage people who are able to travel to Africa to actually go there and immerse themselves in the culture. Even though funds are most definitely needed in order to keep many people in the world alive, your heart is still the most important thing to give. For the heart will sustain. Even far beyond the initial traumatic awareness that there are children actually dying out there.

At times, people have learned to exploit the guilt angle and there have been third world NGOs that have gone past humanitarian ethics.

The following were my reflective thoughts about the concept of Giving:

"Healing comes though Giving. From Giving comes inner peace. From inner peace comes more Love and Compassion. Give the gift of you. Give with love."

The Flow

Dearest Dr. Gazelle,

My take on 2007 is very simple. It was a year of self discovery. A year of increased joy in balance. And mostly a year of meeting a partner in crime. All I can add to your description of our first meeting, in the Meridien, is how I managed to end the misery of one of their chairs while I was dining with Gabriel Stauring of Stop Genocide Now. It must have been injured already, but I gave it the final nudge to the grave.

Gabriel has a similar determination, a joy in playing, just as we do. He's especially crazy about beach football. The Meridien Hotel is always a great place for meeting special people.

Yes, we talked for ten hours straight. It was easy to do. We felt at home and comfortable straight away because we have such similar values and life experiences. Both of us from culturally mixed backgrounds, both involved in humanitarian work, both walkers on the spiritual path. It is a blessing to be with you. Most of the time, be it in a Skype chat or on a dance floor or in your garden or at your family's place, I feel we are in a zone. You told me that seeing the video of Canton had a big impact on you. The synergy of two people out there making the most of their moment in time. Jubilant in enjoying life and its beauty. Seeing the miracle in all people passing by.

The zone.

That feeling that you long for when you know it. That state of mind, heart, and soul that makes you function to the max, that shows the connection with the whole, the larger picture. An example can be while dancing, when you feel the crowd and yourself are flowing together, or while in a meditation when the bodily limits disappear and a unison of hearts appears. Dr. Road Runner, it is a permanent Zone or flow when we are together. It sparkles and shines. It shows and it feels good. Two children out there to learn and enjoy. You and me. In the process trying to invite as many other people as possible to the party.

I made up my mind. I wish to experience the flow again. So I'm packing my bags and coming back to the USA for a whirlwind tour of lectures on what the North can learn from the South. And what the South can learn from the North.

It was about one hundred years ago that Swami Vivekananda came to the USA to spark a similar exchange between the East and West. According to him, the East could learn materialism from the West and the West spirituality from the East. A hundred years down the road, all varieties of ayurveda, yoga, Indian food, and lifestyles can be found in the USA, while values and business ethics imported from the West percolate through the culture of India.

What about a cross-transfusion of values between North and South? On my last tour I kept on talking about resilience, dignity, and humor—values central in the culture of the Zaghawa refugees. What the South may need is transparency, accountability, and a true service mentality of business. Time to exchange those values.

It also means blowing up the barriers that currently exist. We call the world economic markets Free Trade. How does that possibly rhyme with subsidies in the EU and the USA on agricultural products? How is it possible that beef and corn from the USA can be sold in Africa below the market price? Why are there import taxes in place?

Why do military industrial complexes from developed countries still get away with selling arms to countries like Sudan, a place where people are tortured, persecuted and where genocide still happens?

Why do oil companies invest little in local society, sharing only with the elite in power, while taking home their big profits?

Why do we still let men with no heart mismanage African countries for nearly twenty years (Idris Déby, Omar el Bashir)?

Ultimately our lack of caring will boomerang on us. There will be a time when Africa is much better developed, and I am sure the memory will remain of dictators who were supported by the superpowers. Today in Ivory Coast the French have gotten booted out and are treated like second-rate citizens, the result of their backing unpopular dictators for years.

Everywhere you go you can learn so much about human nature. Africa has been a very good learning ground for power versus force, for love versus war, for money versus soul, for good versus evil. Or rather for the ambiguity of man. It is here where you will see the most beautiful gestures man can make, sharing the last of their food, and the worst, refusing to see the value of a life. Killing children, elders, and adults indiscriminately. In one package the ultimate of sacrifice and the ultimate of egoism.

Over the last year I've had the good fortune to meet many people on the crossroads between the two poles of the world. Some come for short visits, some stay to work for decades. But there seems to be a body of people out there who want intercommunication between the people in the South and the people in the North. The Internet is a great tool—Web cams, blogs, videologs, photos, stories. But that is the format. What matters most are the storytellers. And in that resource, Africa is well endowed. Oral history is still the dominant way that the youth learn their cultural tradition. It reminds me often of growing up in India, where a huge body of stories, myths, and histories describes social customs and life.

Every child in India knows the Mahabharata and the Ramayana. And here in different countries the different tribes have their original stories. The storyteller weaves his magic and transfixes the audience, taking away the sense of specific time, place, and person.

Dear Liz,

It is time to weave some stories. I will have to challenge my students of the sixth year to think out loud and tackle public health issues. The class is about to start, and I have prepared, but want to do a bit more, to keep on weaving the material so I share the wisdom and joy.

A big hug today, as every day, until later today or tomorrow.
Dr. Boofalloo

Impact for Change

Meridien Chari, N'Djamena, 19, 22, and 23 January 2008

Hi Dr. Road Runner,

I have returned to the Hotel Meridien, back to the swimming pool where we first met face-to-face. I'm in need of a cool head, a plunge in the pool, an opportunity to talk with like-minded souls. It seems that when you open your mind and heart, the seekers pop up.

I've been thinking lately about the question: "What is the biggest impact you as a person could have on the world as it is now, and how could the world change in the next twenty years because of your steps?"

A question hurled at me yesterday was similar in spirit. What one thing motivates you so much, you could let go of every other desire or ambition until you have achieved the one goal? What unique thing makes you tick? Well … err … hmm.

It got me thinking. About six months ago I compiled several of my goals.

Teach public health at a university in Africa.

Work in a hospital in Africa.

Raise awareness about Chad and Sudan.

Head a local nongovernmental organization.

Write a book and a blog.

Currently I am working on each one of those goals. That feels good. The truth, however, is that my deepest convictions are only being partly addressed. Sharing the utmost of joy, connecting of souls, being a living bridge between East and West, North and South. Standing on the crossroad and encouraging exchange of views, experience, thoughts, knowledge, attitude, practices. Living the moment!

Humanity has an infinite capacity for goodness. And it also has, at the same time, a tendency to be distracted from benign living. The path is to demonstrate being the change you want to see. It is not about achieving goals as postulated above, but about each and every moment of life being in a state of bliss. What is the point of teaching about hygienic customs to prevent diarrheal disease when you do not treat fellow beings with respect and love? Just now I remembered how roughly I treated a man coming to sell me some magazines. All because I had received a string of bad news by Internet. The poor man confronted me a couple of days later about my boorish behavior, and I had to agree with him. The path to bliss requires each and every act to be brimful of mindful conscience and good intent. I still have a lot to learn. The recurring themes for me are patience and acceptance. And that is the answer to the question.

The essence of being is giving the utmost to reach the ultimate positive potential. The childlike state of bliss. It goes way beyond work, vocation, family, and friends. It is the state of mind that leads you to love the unlovable and treat all beings with equal measures of love and respect.

A steep task. Every moment being the best you can be. But a very rewarding one. The obstacles that seem to appear on your path and within yourself are the steppingstones toward a deeper understanding and connection.

Dr. Gazelle,

Somehow the last week I have not been able to send what I've written. But we talked on the phone. Talked a lot. Talked about opportunities on the path. Talked about crossroads. Laughed. Talked about some of the struggles in Chad. Where to focus? What is utmost priority?

Be in the moment.

Let go and the solution will come to you. The path clears up when you unclutter the mind. Worrying or stressing will lead to hair loss and loss of sleep. Both manes and sleep are required, so be in the moment.

The path.

As if it was meant to be. I called the doctor in UNICEF who is our contact person and got the unfortunate response that until further notice he will be too busy. There is currently a polio epidemic in Chad, so they are focusing on that and that only. The answer has come. This afternoon I am arranging a trip to the South for five days, and afterward I am off to India. First week of February, I can make it to some STAND conferences in the USA taking place during the weekends. Kick-starting my trip to the USA while talking with the future leaders of the nation. Those with the heart to stand up, care, and make a difference.

In the process I will rewrite our project proposal for Africa Vision over the next week so it gives a crystal clear overview of the needs, the opportunities, and a comprehensible plan of action, with a pilot project component and a budget.

A few days hanging out with Mr. Tree and Mr. Forest, two friends who are visiting me now, have been fun and insightful. Their business model is a community-based, value-added model focusing on sustainability. Let us take a public health intervention as an example. The needs of a village in Longone Orientale are massive. The vaccination coverage is varying from 0 to 50 percent, but should be 95 percent. Children die of several preventable diseases, including malaria, diarrhea, measles, and lower respiratory tract infections. There are many people in the villages stricken by blindness due to various causes like cataracts, vitamin A deficiency, and trachoma. There is a lack of medication, qualified medical staff, materials, transportation, and lack of infrastructure.

The opportunities are clear and evident. A monthly mobile vaccination clinic could lift the vaccination coverage to acceptable levels. Another route would be supplying the health care centers with the stock of vaccines and the petrol to keep their fridges working. The opportunities for blindness are in two fields—cure and prevention. Cure would mean a $30 cataract operation by use of an intraocular lens. Trachoma requires antibiotic treatment, and in severe cases an operation. But there is a role for preventive medicine as well, and it is just as important. Flies cause infection of the eyes in trachoma, so improved hygienic and sanitation practices would have a major impact on eye health. So would dietary measures, or supplying vitamin A, which is usually deficient here.

Malaria can be overcome by early recognition, and treatment from the local health workers who follow a specific training module. Impregnated bed nets reduce transmission, and as long as the use is clearly monitored and explained they are known to work well. For diarrhea, introduction of early recognition and treatment with oral rehydration solution is the difference between life and death. For measles there is a very efficient vaccine. Chest infection can be combated with early diagnosis and simple antibiotics.

There is a shortage of village health workers, nurses, and doctors. In the smaller villages you will be lucky to find a motivated and qualified health worker who has access to medication. The same goes for finding a nurse. In bigger cities it is still not easy to find a doctor who has access to the basic needs to do his or her work.

For most communities, proper health care access has been out of reach for a long time. An incentive for them is helping out with supplies, training modules on a triage system, and a small financial award. It is the paradigm swing that requires a belief that with a little bit of help and focus, the ten most common health issues can be addressed in an affordable and sustainable way. That their physical, political, and economic contribution can make a major impact on the health of their elders and youths. That a healthier future is possible by increasing positive health practices and working on reducing practices that have a negative impact. No one should be left behind, and trying to make it work in one of the poorest countries in the world, marred by civil strife and corruption, is only a challenge that will show it is possible anywhere. All of us hope for a better future for the children.

In India, Liz, a doctor couple, Bang and Bang, worked with a similar approach. They sought out in poor communities those people that did remarkably well. They did in-depth studies of what knowledge, attitudes, and practices those people had that made such a positive impact on their health and their family's health. They called this kind of behavior "positive defiance." Each of these families had survival strategies that the less successful families did not have.

For example, one family would eat dark green vegetables growing by the roadside. Another family knew what crabs were nutritious, and used them to supplement their diet. These lessons were bundled. The positive defiant experience was shared with the other parents in the village, in class settings. For each and every different environment there are different behavioral patterns that give a positive outcome. Human creativity shines through.

So, Dr. Gazelle, besides imposing on communities what is known to work. Vaccinations or vitamin A supplements or deworming or ORS. There should always be a huge component to appreciate that knowledge, that attitude, and that practice that works very well for the positive deviants in that environmental setting.

Local problems require local solutions by local communities with local resources, aided by international experience.

Experiencing the Human Condition

N'Djamena, 23 January 2008

The path to the utmost, the childlike state of bliss, is not straight. Much maya, illusion, and distraction around.

Letting go!

Being!

Being the change you want to see in the world.

Dabbling around, absorbing as much as humanly possible.

Playing, and learning about the human spirit.

Experiencing the human condition in its worst and best moments. There is a realization that within scarcity there is abundance. That those having near to nothing in a material sense may be all the richer for it in a spiritual sense. Not a rule hewn in stone, but in general seen in the areas around the world where I have worked. The most beautiful smiles are abundant. Laughter is plentiful. A hug or an embrace is the norm. There is time and a place to listen to stories and songs.

When distractions like television, Internet, and material want are to a minimum, life seems to be about what it could be about.

Being, not being confused by illusions. No! Being and walking the path in a childlike state of bliss. Illuminating the illusion and distraction away. Being in the moment. Living the real deal. Balancing the edge.

It seems that when certain basics are available (food, water, shelter, and security), humans are at a level of serenity. It seems that when more is added (advertisement-driven consumption, such as holidays, cars, a second house, electronics, fancy clothes), humans struggle to reach that inner peace. Despite blossoming spas, retreat centers, yoga schools, and many more forms of self-searching, the easiest road (or perhaps the hardest road in some ways), turning inward through meditation is overlooked. Focusing on the road to self has a divine potential.

In my belief, all the good that I was presented in a loving way by my parents is part and parcel of being. Trying to reach the ultimate of love for all mankind, truthfulness in all matters, is the foundation of being. Within self the unison with the planet can be found. All you need to do is listen to the inner child. It will show the way to bliss and back. Creating a playful path. Yes, obstacles will be on that road. We will have to overcome. Obstacles may also be seen as opportunities to grow. I have mentioned several of the points in my character which are my opportunities for growth. And day by day, moment by moment, I am working on them. There have been some moments of regression, and also some spectacular moments of growth. Moments of self-delusion, as when I thought at age eighteen or twenty-five that I was pretty much God's gift to mankind. Near perfection. I do not feel ashamed to write this today, but my, what a self-delusion. It must have been unbearable for those around me. Yet you live, you learn.

Every moment today I am grateful. Grateful to still have a flexible mind that recognizes that everything, all belief, can change by deep pondering, or just as likely by flashes of insight. Each and every person on the planet has a very unique story to tell and a lesson to teach you. Continuous growth is the ultimate path to insight. Understanding comes from gurus and seers as well. If you are open to it, at several points in your life the right person will come by to give you insight, to help you along. And the great thing is that at the same time you yourself may be seen by some people as a (divine) inspiration, a sounding board. The one that brings courage to make decisions.

Soul

Dr. Gazelle,

You have been more than a muse to me. A muse inspires, but it seems that whenever together we set the house on fire. The combined love for playfulness, sharing the love, uplifting, and caring. Similar minds and kindred hearts aiming for the utmost. In India when you meditate for days and days to Lord Brahma it is called *tapas*. The outcome of that penance and meditation is to receive a boon or a wish more in the stride of Ali Baba. My wish would have been a soul mate. And guess what, Liz? I did not even have to do penance, and look what I got ...

The Internet connection has been killing me of late. To get some synchronicity going, I wish I could see your latest writing. Then again, I believe in karma. This story will flow as it is. The connection will be there either way.

Got to give time to time.

Be-ing

25 January 2008

Dearest Dr. Rainbow,
Be.
Be the moment.
Be the Light.
Be the hope.
Be the music.
Be the gift.
Be love.

These words came to my mind as I read your heartwarming insights and wisdom from your recent daily life experiences. The image of your stethoscope on that baby's chest—the child who was already dead—still haunts me. My heart goes out to the child's family, and to you, who had to deliver the message that their child was gone. And to pull from within you the ability to be compassionate toward those who do things that seem so horrific. Love the lovable and the unlovable. No matter what we do as physicians, it is difficult to forget who the true Healer is. Especially when little children die. We know in the depths of our souls who the commander–in-chief of life or death really is. And it is not you or me. What a relief there is in knowing this. That we don't have to be in control of everything. For we truly are not in control anyway. Sometimes we just think we want to be. Human.

To live in the moment and to be the moment. Time is man-made. The Algonquin Indians certainly believed that there is no such thing as time. So does it mean that a moment actually even exists? For a moment is time-based. Paul Tillich's *The Courage to Be* addresses the issues of being. He wrote that the "power of being is identified with virtue (not time), and virtue, consequently, with essential nature."

A seven-year-old boy who recently came into my office was a bit timid. Then once he got used to things, and realized I was pretty benign and would not give him a shot, he started to move constantly and continuously. He delighted in climbing everywhere. He impulsively and aggressively shoved the stuffed animal lizard in our faces—to "kiss" his mother and me. His movements were erratic, aggressive, and brusque. As the mother started to talk about domestic violence and how the child's father beat her up, the child's behaviors escalated to a point of requiring some very firm limit setting and calm-down techniques. He started hitting and pounding the stuffed animals, yelling, "If you don't behave, I'm going to whoop you so badly that you will hurt until you die." The mother's eyes got bigger. She disclosed later that those were exactly the words that the child's father would say to her. Clearly, the violence had gotten embedded in the child's mind. She got flustered, and then she started to cry. This seemed to make the boy more hyperactive. It took a while for him to eventually calm down. Yet nevertheless, he did. The mother required comforting. Post-traumatic agony. Anything can trigger the painful memories. The mind short-circuits and starts to relive the past as if it was present.

My point? What does it mean for a child and a mother who suffered so much abuse to live in the moment? How can they be the moment?

Appreciations

30 January 2008, Back in Louisville from NYC

Dear Dr. Rainbow,

Sitting in a very Zen-like restaurant in NYC, I thought about you. And wished we could have been sitting there together, like we did in Heartbeat Restaurant, just talking about what we believe are the possible solutions to many world problems. So many things have happened. This time I stayed in a hotel close to the Hudson River, so I had to get a cab to midtown Manhattan. Observing people traveling through Grand Central Station, the trains, the city streets, the cabs, has become more fascinating to me. And meeting people from all over the world—a taxi driver from Russia, another cabbie from Pakistan, a lady from Ecuador, another from Canada, a saleslady from Ethiopia, and three young girls from Puerto Rico. My visit with my son went reasonably well. It is always great to exchange I-love-yous and hugs when we visit.

One of our mutual friends was already waiting at the Capital Grille restaurant by the time I got there for dinner. She truly is an adorable, bright, and dynamic lady. A lady with a vision to uplift the world with appreciations. We talked about many ideas and merged our thoughts on the site DailyAppreciations.net. A place to acknowledge all the things in life that you appreciate, and through the sentences you post, to strengthen your positive thinking. What if people posted their appreciations on the DA site when they were feeling down and out? Would this help reverse their energy level and better their emotional state?

My experience is that the more appreciations I post daily, the lighter I begin to feel. Almost like a rush of endorphins starts happening after ten appreciations. A paradigm shift in the mind. What would happen within a company if employees posted appreciations in between their work time? Would that help prevent burnout? Would learning how to appreciate more lead to more productivity?

Sunday morning I met up with our friend and her sister for brunch at a little luncheonette in the city. Her sister is bright and delightful, and reminded me so much of my sister Marissa. At one point we were laughing so loudly that a lady came up to us and asked us, essentially, to pipe down. We initially could not believe it. The luncheonette was already very noisy, apart from our laughter. Since she was offended, we all just apologized.

My thought—what must someone feel when hearing such gut-level laughter? I wondered if she may have been depressed and may have reacted to the laughter itself. Maybe it reminded her that she was too unhappy to enjoy herself. Or perhaps we were just having such a good time that we could not hear our own voices anymore.

When I left my hotel to meet these ladies, a burly uniformed doorman who was built like a football player was kind enough to flag a taxicab for me. As I hurriedly walked toward the cab, I suddenly noticed a white plastic bag floating on the wind, from out of nowhere. As the doorman opened the cab's door, a gust of wind pushed the bag down exactly where my feet were going. I fell forward. Such an awkward, startling feeling. My face and jaw smashed into the doorman's chest. Fortunately, he had the instinct to turn around and catch me. If he had not, I would have fallen literally flat on my face on the cab door or pavement. The cab driver said he saw everything that happened and that he almost had a heart attack watching me fall. All through the ride to midtown he kept reiterating that the doorman had saved my life. The doorman's name: Armando Garcia. I told him that I would write about him in our book. Thank you, Armando. Earth angel.

While in the plane, I was reading a simple inspirational book by Gay Hendricks. It encouraged the reader to ponder one simple question. That on our deathbed, we look back at our lives and ask ourselves: was our life a success?

If not, then what would we have wished for to make our life a success? A question so simple, yet sublime. I pondered this throughout the flight back from NYC to Louisville. It allowed me to think about my priorities in life again. Life can go so fast. With a blink of an eye. My destiny would have been quite different if the doorman had not stopped my sudden fall.

This thought brings me back to you, Dr. Buffalo. What does it truly mean to live in the moment? Does it mean living the moment with a meaningful purpose? Using the moment for whatever comes our way? To do whatever we want to do?

The eye camps are certainly needed there in Africa. Your public health background can have a strong, uplifting impact on all the crucial problems affecting the refugees in Chad. And contaminated water is certainly a huge problem there, too. What a relief to know that the United Nations is now making clean water for the world their number one agenda. That to me is good news.

We are now revving up in mobilizing people to join us in the Healthy and Safe Water for the World International Conference in Mubende, Uganda, in July, 2008. The Rural Health Care Foundation will be the grassroots leaders there. The idea is to create a mega-voice from the various splintered water groups and individuals interested in raising awareness about clean and safe water for the world. The important thing is to get people there to immerse, and come face-to-face with the people of Uganda.

Some may say, why not just donate the amount we plan to use for the trip? The idea, however, is, to invest in the education of people, to raise their awareness directly. To meet friends who live on the other side of the world. To touch their hearts. For our hearts to be touched. That is what will sustain across time. Connected hearts of people from across the ocean, all working on making good things happen out there. Ongoing. Not a onetime guilt-giving donation. Something more lasting. After experiencing Africa, my life has never been the same.

Utmost experience.

How Many Soul Mates?

Souls. Soul mates. Across time and space. I once asked you, how many soul mates can one have in a lifetime? And you said: maybe, if there is oneness, then everyone is a soul mate. Then you said that maybe we can have a different soul mate each day. And then you said that perhaps within all that, people like you and I may well be energy-calibrated so similarly that the answer is back to one.

I don't know the answers. Yet I am thankful to know that in praying for a soul mate you ended up getting me. And even sans penance. Just meditation. Hmmmm ... I wonder what would happen if you went through your penance? We do blaze some trails out there together, don't we? The utmost love for all.

Living in the Moment

N'Djamena, 31 January 2008

Dearest Liz,

You ask about living in the moment. Well let me describe what is going on in N'Djamena right now. The air is thick with the noise of choppers taking off. The main street has been like a Russian parade of military hardware. Dozens of jeeps loaded with men, rocket-propelled grenades and guns, several tanks, and the heavy artillery rolling out toward the outskirts of town.

This is not an exercise. Rumors have been buzzing for more than a week now. Rebels—or freedom fighters, depending on which point of view you wish to take—have been creeping up toward town. The oil companies have evacuated their expatriate staff, all foreigners have been advised to stay in, schools, banks are closed. N'Djamena is preparing for a clash.

The people here are used to the threat, but there is some panic with groups of Cameroonians pouring out of town to their native place across the bridge. The sentiment I feel on the street is one of acceptance. This happens once or twice a year; it does not really matter which dictator is in charge. They will enrich themselves and run the country into the ground. What to do?

How to live in the moment?

I am writing, for one answer to that question. And I have been thinking about my trip to India and the USA. Brainstorming on the different presentations and discovering the program keynote Apple-based, which will help me make a smooth presentation, or actually two.

I decided to make different presentations tailored to different audiences. One aimed at talking about what we, as a general audience in the West, can learn from the Sudanese that have gone through hell. And how they still radiate resilience, humor, and dignity. The second one for medical people working and enjoying public health service in a refugee camp.

So there may be a major clash near the city between rebels and the military tonight, and I am writing and planning what I could do for the medical faculty. I was skyping with some friends to keep my mind calm. Am I worried? No. Am I a bit tense? Violence and combat is something I have already experienced close up in Burundi, Nepal, and Chad, and it is never a relaxed ride. But I won't worry about a thing, 'cause every little thing is going to be all right.

In Nepal I had the experience of being in Kathmandu when the crown prince, with or without help, managed to wipe out nearly the entire dynasty. Riot police rushed into the disco to look for possible accomplishes to the massacre and *lathis*—bamboo clubs bound in iron—were wielded freely. I carried a young man who had been smashed on the head to a health clinic, passing through the line of policemen by explaining that I was a doctor and this young man needed urgent care. Automatic pilot, I never looked back. On the same day, several people got killed in fights between the riot police and crowds of mourners. Hectic times. You do what you need to do.

The next day on the street was one of the most intense days I have ever experienced. The king in Nepal is revered by about half of the people as the reincarnation of Vishnu. Beyond human, therefore. And even though Nepali people never cry in public, thousands of them were crying that day. Hundreds of thousands of supporters of the king had shaved their heads to show their grief. You could feel the sorrow in the air. Heavy and deep sorrow. At the same time, the other half of the country supports the Maoist rebel movement. So those people were relieved by the auto-destruction of the royal family. Their troops were nearing the capital Kathmandu as well. It did not take much longer for them to eventually get into the prime power-wielding position.

Just act, Liz. You know the feeling. Just do it. Tomorrow, if there are massive amounts of casualties, I shall slip into my scrubs, wrap a stethoscope around my neck, and lend a hand in the medical clinic. This is Chad, however. Let us see whether the rebels came here to negotiate or to fight. Everything is possible here.

The abused child and mother you write about have gone through horrible experiences. Something you would wish does not happen on this planet. Yet it is remarkably common. Men beating women and children. Abuse on all levels emotional, sexual, physical, and social.

How can they be in the moment?

Utmost

They are survivors. In a way they have found mechanisms to keep on going. In my limited experience with people who have gone through the most horrible of experiences, there is an enormous regenerating capacity of human nature. The most loving and resilient, with a sense of humor and dignity, are often those that have gone through rape, or the forced viewing of murder of children and husband.

Clearly, this miracle does not always happen; many cannot cope with what they've undergone. But it is amazing to see how many people still have dreams. You may take away a house, cattle, the lives of loved ones, land. You may kick people out of their homes, chase them with big guns and airplanes. You can never take away dreams.

The human soul can endure. The most despicable acts cannot be forgotten, but they can be forgiven. The mother and child you write about, Liz, may have been given a rough deal, and out of that sadness may come the most beautiful growth. If you have seen hell from inside, is there not a big opportunity to live life as if in heaven, given the presence of loving, accepting, caring people around you?

I am not pleading for all of us to live a life of abusive parents or neighbors, but it makes living in the moment the only possibility. Either that, or drown in the pain.

Do we do whatever we want to do?

I believe not. Things and people are dropped on the path. Some are in the guise of an obstacle, some appear as an opportunity. And as I wrote before, all obstacles are stepping-stones, opportunities to grow. A path of following your destiny is called *karmayoga* in India. It is one of the paths toward the Divine. Do what comes on your path. Be guided by the Divine inspiration and all will be well.

I appreciate this day, this moment. As it is nothing more and nothing less. Because I am writing, because I am flexing the mind, because I will hit the endorphin wall if I keep appreciating. Indeed, a friend of ours has taken great steps to create the website www.dailyappreciations.org. It is a great way to whisk a smile back on your face. First, by reading so many positive entries, and secondly because after a short while of writing those entries you do indeed feel like you are flying.

I appreciate all the appreciators in the website and the founding members for their time, energy, and shared love. It is a great laugh and a fine learning experience. Appreciating as a way to get the world around you into a brighter light. Giving a compliment was something I struggled with for a long time. And receiving one was even harder. With the second I am still not doing great, but the first has become more and more easy through the website. Clearly there is a big impact in how you approach people. With a smile on your face you can get away with nearly everything. And a smile and an appreciation is better than a flower and chocolate. Just imagine all four of them together.

The Siege

1 February 2008

Dearest Ashis,

Siege. N'Djamena. Sending you a protective sacred white light all around you, Dr. Buffalo. Being there side by side with you, tending and serving those who are hurt or suffering, seems much better than wondering how you are doing there. You know what I mean, Ashis. Be the Light and Peace in the eye of the storm. Your instincts and compassion will serve you well. And as you and I know too well, both of us seem to find that inner peace and tranquility under fire. Perhaps that is another reason why we do the work we do. Only God knows for certain.

I missed three of your Skype calls, which compelled me to call you back after I got home from work. Receiving your last writings reminded me of the nobility of your spirit. The *Sudan Tribune*

News wrote about how there are now one thousand French troops there and that the rebels have surrounded N'Djamena. This is reminiscent of April, 2006.

Your mom and I have been skyping. As a mom myself, I know how she feels about knowing that her son is in a predicament. Yet she has serenity and faith. My grandmothers were the same way. Their faith shows us that we are all exactly where we need to be. There is a tremendous irrational force within me that makes me want to fly there now, right where you are. No different from when I went there before—not necessarily because I can do so much for anyone, but more because it is the kind of situation where the opportunity to serve is at its utmost. And to serve right alongside a comrade of the soul. But don't worry. For now, I shall hold my horses. And pray. And meditate.

Your thoughts about living in the moment are well received.

Living in the moment does not always mean that we are bright-eyed and bushy-tailed. Nor does it mean that we are lacking extreme emotions, whether bliss or discomfort. Living in the moment can mean the utmost immersion into a given experience. The experiences can range from the most mundane to the most extraordinary.

What defines it as living in the moment? Being the moment. When we transcend and give at full throttle all our senses and awareness about an experience. When we feel beyond our senses and beyond our heart of hearts. When we respond with our souls and discover gratitude, joy, and beauty in every breath our spirit takes. When every breath we take is the alpha and the omega. When we are enlightened by the utmost realization that we are in the heart of God and that God is in our souls.

Appreciations uplift the spirits. And there are many ways to express appreciations. Not only in words, though honest loving words can be powerful healers. Giving flowers, chocolates, and teddy bears are about symbolic and palpable appreciations. The value of these tangible appreciations depends on the depth of love and gratitude that the giver and the receiver have for one another. I love giving all kinds of appreciations. An appreciative hug and cuddle are special. And yes indeed. I, too, appreciate all the appreciators in DailyAppreciations.org. They believe that expressing appreciation can raise the world's positive energy, and they act on their belief.

Ashis dear,

Le Hotel Meridien has been a seat of lovely memories, so I am happy that you are there right now. I can still visualize us dancing with total abandon by the poolside.

You say that it is heating up there. I can only imagine. Keep staying in touch and stay close. We are all exactly where we need to be, so there must be a strong reason why you are there now. Most likely to be a Light for many. Nevertheless, it will be wonderful to know that as soon as there are international flights, you will grab the next flight out of there. Stay free in your mind though the circumstances constrict. May God bless you and guide you, Dr. Buffalo. And feel the love that we all have for you. Whispering you prayers across the ocean. Praying for Chad and the Chadians. Keep still, our hearts.

Love, Ashis, love.

Dr. Gazelle

Utmost

N'Djamena, February 2 2008

Dearest Dr. Gazelle,

Stranded just three days before a long-desired trip to India. Life can deal you strange hands. Yes, Liz, as I write this I am in a besieged town where rebels are in the process of booting out the dictator of the past nineteen years. This is history in the making. It has gone down in the most gruesome way. There are hundred and perhaps thousands of deaths on both sides. Vicious fighting! Hundreds of jeeps on both sides. Throw in some tanks and helicopters and we can create mighty fireworks. The battle took place fifty kilometers from the capital, and it seemed that the rebels would have a hard time to enter the town.

Today, however, it became obvious that they would invade with ease. For the last twelve hours we have been getting used to artillery fire, tanks shooting, guns bursting, grenades exploding, helicopter gunships flying over, and troops fighting in front of the hotel. At one point, some troops entered the hotel and shattered the main entry. About forty of us huddled in the kitchen, hearing the bullets ricochet on the inner walls. Yet there was a certain tranquility in the moment. Most people still behind in the hotel reacted reasonably, especially considering that with less thick walls it may have easily been their end. I am so grateful we have a group of brave French military protecting the perimeter. They didn't respond until they were shot at, but their return fire made the attackers disappear. None of them were wounded, as if by a miracle. Later in the day a tank took a potshot at the hotel, and so did a heavy machine gun. A young Japanese man had eight bullets fly through his room and instantly he ran out with a pillow wrapped around his head.

I have mixed feelings about being here today. Stress about what could happen. Worries about friends living in N'Djamena. But overall I have been grateful. Grateful to be alive to witness this moment of history. Grateful that in times of extreme distress I can still go around with a smile on my face. Hugging those who need it. Singing songs with those who are stressed. Writing freely about how I feel about this. Being worried to a certain extent. Having great discussions about the present and future of different African nations. Meditating during shelling. That was a great feeling. Just letting go of the violence and immersing into love, praying for a peaceful outcome.

When your life is on the line there is but one thing to do.

Be.

Accept whatever happens. This was a very insightful moment. A moment that for a little while the ego could be transcended. A moment of realization, of inner peace.

I am so happy to live. I am going to dance some more, as soon as I can. And even if I need to stay in the French military base for some days, eventually I will be able to make it to India. There I can reflect some more on what it means to be so close to the gates of death yet again.

Balancing the edge, I think it is called.

All the more reason to go to the USA and explain the plight of the Chadians. Today in the kitchen I see their remarkable humor, dignity, and resilience yet again. None of the Chadians seems to be worried. And why would they? They have been through this nonsense for a long time now, and it does not look like it will change anytime soon.

What can I learn from the Chadians?

Living the utmost.

When under pressure, people show their inner strength. Nobody here has complained or panicked. Everybody is grateful. Sleeping on mats in the bar. Watching television while the mortars pound outside. The children playing on the floor of the kitchen. So used to unfolding events. The staff of the Meridien is running its operation as if there is no problem. Three days steady now. And we are all calm because of that.

My departure for India I planned several weeks ago to be on the third of February. Life throws obstacles, steppingstones, and opportunities on the path. To learn. To shake the shackles. To come back to center point.

Six years ago I came to work in Africa for the first time. The continent has gotten into my heart, under my skin, and into my blood. Today I have felt the pain of Africa. An old friend, the owner Ali Baba, one of my favorite local restaurants, came to tell me his story. He and five of his staff had to endure battles between tanks and jeeps armed with rocket-propelled grenades. All they could hide in was the backroom kitchen. All walls were riddled with bullets and the roof was about to collapse. He had just sent his wife and daughter away, and five minutes later had seen a tank rolling down the street. Our street. In the process of telling me about the fight, he informed me that my apartment got hit by a rocket. I am so happy that I left the house when I did. Who cares about the paperwork? The material possessions? What I am worried about is my friends. Not only for the risk of stray bullets, but even more for the looters that have been terrorizing the neighborhood.

I had a feeling that things were turning nasty so I grabbed my passport and took off for the Meridien just in time. No other transport has been available until now. My Indian friends, however, have to roll with it. People suffer under the burden of dictators. Many houses in town have been destroyed. Looting is on the way.

This afternoon we were evacuated by armored vehicles in a convoy. Twenty minutes to reach the French base. A ride taken in a state of meditation. We have been so lucky so far. Nobody got hurt in the hotel, and all got evacuated. I met several people here at the French military base who lost their entire house and all their paperwork.

Imagine if you are Chadian. All the foreigners may be evacuated but how about my Indian friends? Faizal, his wife, his kid, Bechir, and Mooni. There is no protection for them. We are flown off to Gabon, and from there we disperse to all places in the world. We shall be out of the deep hole Chad has dug itself in.

I am thinking about my little street urchins, my next-door neighbors. They live in a tent. How will that protect them from stray bullets and grenades? Or Dr. Djada, the dean of the medical faculty. Will he be operating full-time to save the eyesight of soldiers, or is he trying to assure the security of his family? Many Chadians live in simple housing. How did they overcome the heavy tank and artillery fire of the rebels? Will the rebels be any better to the local population than the current government has been?

That remains to be seen, but many of them have served their terms in the nineteen-year stretch of this government's rule. It is not likely there will be any change for the average Joe in the street. I am off to Gabon, West Africa, this evening or tomorrow morning. From there it is likely I will fly to Paris, and there I can start organizing money and paperwork, I hope. My departure from the house was done in a bit of a hurry.

Gratitude is what I feel today.

Today I live.

I will return to Chad. This country needs it as much as ever. Thank you, French military.

Thank you, dear Krishna, for protecting all the people in the hotel.

Let me pray that you can protect as many people as possible in Chad.

Chad deserves better.

In the French military base, all comes together. I find a bed (a sewer cover), and a Turkish carpet materializes out of nothing, then a blanket and a pair of shoes. I feel like I have a magic lamp. Our flight out of Chad will be tomorrow morning, I hope. For now, the fire is just sporadic, fortunately.

The rebels may have left town to intercept a group of government-friendly fighters coming in from the East.

N'Djamena-Libreville (Gabon), 4 February 2008

Dr. Gazelle,

I followed my hunch and it was right. When it does not feel good, act. Be swift before it is too late. I took my last possibility for a ride; even if I forgot some essential stuff, I did not forget myself. Africa makes you feel alive. Joy and sorrow, heartbeat to heartbeat. As I am praying for my friends, I am happy to breathe in and out calmly. Everything will be sorted out. I love this life, and will be back for more. Risks such as dying on the job do cross my mind once in a while, but if it is supposed to happen it will, and in the meantime I will go on doing what I love to do.

How else to live?

Balance the edge and tip it once in a while. Sniff and experience life in its deepest misery! Being shelled by artillery is scary business. Bullets whizzing by make you wonder why you are here again. Yet, as I said before, nobody got hurt in the hotel. Somehow good can happen even in the worst of environments.

Once I get access to the mobile network I might find out what has happened to my friends. And what has happened to N'Djamena. It has been said that large parts of it have been flattened, and that there are many civilian casualties.

I have been going through this whole ordeal with friends—Mr. Tree, Mr. Forest, Gabriel, and Katie-J (the latter two are from the StopGenocideNow.org team). And all of us have gone through the experience in a different way, yet all of us are calm. As they do not speak French very well, I've had the good fortune to translate a lot that happens. I have talked with many people—Tunisians, French, Americans, and Canadians. All have their own perspective. Shared aromas and different tastes. Fear and excitement, sorrow and the elation of being alive. All the emotions one can think of have come up for them in recent days. What has surprised me most is the amount of positive energy around. Hugs and supportive words. Silly games and dialogue.

Gabriel and Katie-J have been role-model citizen journalists. Posting online on YouTube their experience of the attack on Hotel Meridien, and their commentary. Doing interviews with the BBC and other news agencies. Their presence is of massive importance because very few journalists had access to the Internet after the satellite connections shut down. The first thing to go was the mobile phone network. Mr. Tree and Mr. Forest did their share of filming as well. And they will upload their stuff rapidly as well. Myself, I am writing blogs, writing on Utmost. Talking with people about the current conflict. Planning to come back as soon as possible.

Why come back to Chad when you have gone through what we have just gone through? Imagine the needs of the Chadian. Imagine how sad it must feel to have one clan fighting over the resources your entire country produces, trying to swallow it whole. Imagine the impact simple interventions like cataract operations can have in this country. Imagine that you can live your dream.

Right now I am in a French military transport airplane, on the way to Gabon. I had the pleasure to listen to Deepak Chopra, Wayne Dyer, and a talk on gratitude. Experiencing the overflowing abundance in my life has been great today. What do you really need to be happy?

I always want to travel with one small bag. All else is superfluous. Makes life more comfortable but it is perhaps just as good to do more with less. As I entered Chad this time I arrived with only 60 kilograms (about 130 pounds), an amount that has always felt as if it was too much. Bottom line is that it really was too much. Not because it got hit by rocket fire or got looted afterward. No, just because I feel just as happy without. Practically it means less books (more focus and time to write my own books), less clothes (less choice the better), less gizmos (mmm ... here I am starting to think. Given my inclination to go for photos and video blogging, perhaps I should give in.) What I will miss is the Eagle Head made by Reggie that your sister Marissa gave me, and the key to the city of Louisville. Highly symbolic, but I like them a lot.

It is not confirmed that all is gone. But with the amount of looting and the potential battle breaking out over N'Djamena, it is likely that my house will go down and that all my belongings will be taken. The practicalities can be sorted out. Vaccination booklet and driver's license are gone. It will be fun to explain to my city hall that my papers were either destroyed by rocket fire in a failed coup in Chad, or looted as a consequence of the battle.

Praise the Internet. I have been able to inform my parents and near and dear ones three times over the last three days that I am doing OK. Tonight a further update will follow. So my near and dear are informed and I am OK. More than OK. My ticket out to India was two days after the last flight. There is a reason for that. This has been a humbling experience and a reconfirmation that I am working in the right place. It is where I feel at home. Where I know the needs are. A step on the path to shed to the superfluousness of the ego, baby steps toward transcendence.

Yet focus is required. I need to come up with an intelligible and salable (or, rather, socially marketable) public health-related idea to help out the people of Chad. Without money it has been difficult to get started. Now I see a path, an opportunity. Especially when a lot of the infrastructure of the capital of Chad has been torn apart.

One of the questions is whether good men and women with talent will stay in Chad. Too much has happened. Then again, looking at how many coups and clashes they have already been through, it would not make sense if they leave now.

Will the country slide further down the ladder into a deep dark hole? And if so, are there interventions that need to be done despite all of that? Is it worth taking risks doing mobile eye or other public health clinics? I would strongly argue for taking those risks.

Chadians have consistently been let down by their government and the international community for over twenty-seven years. It has been on the slide for a long time, and the ten million people living there deserve better. Most are not involved in all the fighting and killing. They just suffer from it. So the cause could be uplifting public health aspects in Chad. Helping with books, lectures, training curricula, projectors for the medical faculty. Perhaps the well-stocked library (250 books) has been looted. It remains to be seen, and I still have not been able to contact any of my friends (Chadian or Indian). It ties in with one of my main desires in life: permanent learning and teaching.

Dearest Liz,
It has been a shaky but beautiful ride once again.
Balancing the edge.
Embracing the moment.
Breathing in freedom.
Stepping closer to letting go.
Meditating under artillery barrage.
Comforting scared fellow travelers.
Traveling with the bare minimum (plus Mac).
All you need is a belief that all will be good.

The Siege

4 February 2008

Dear Ashis,

It was painful to see the video, to hear startling, repetitive blasts from machine guns and what seem to be rockets while you, Gabriel, and the StopGenocide.org team duck, deploy, crawl, run, and seek cover within the walls and floors of the Hotel Meridien. Those bullets seemed to be flying all around you there. The saving grace was the video that showed you, Gabriel, and the team being escorted by the French military in a tank. All of you appeared to maintain your peace, and that was good to see. Peace under fire. We both seem to be at our utmost peace under the most disastrous of situations, don't we? Precisely why we do what we do. I won't even begin to analyze that one for now. But it won't take a rocket-scientist/psychiatrist to understand what that is all about after they know both of us.

Helplessness is a tough feeling. Watching friends, people we love and care for, look death straight in the eye. Just one bullet. A stray rocket. Some erratic shrapnel. In that instant, it could have been all over. Yet you were spared. Which means there is more for you to do for our world. This whole experience also reminds us of our powerlessness, and who is truly in charge and in control.

It is not either one of us, that is for sure.

Imagining what may have been happening seems more difficult than actually knowing what is going on. So the videos gave me some internal relief. At the same time, it gave me chills to see the beautiful Hotel Meridien, the place where we first met, relaxed, and danced around its pool, turned into a war zone. Most of all because you were right there, along with other humanitarian friends.

A big part of me wished I was there too, fully knowing that disastrous times like that are opportunities in disguise to serve others. I know that sounds odd, but that is the way I feel. When I first tried to call the hotel, and actually got through, the person who answered was guarded and hesitant. He talked to someone else, and then told me that you were not there. Later, when I called again, I got through but the phone rang for a long time before anyone answered. That was when I knew that something was wrong. That was when I started to contact people who I thought could help.

Backup. I thought about the exit routes, like going to Cameroon, being with the French, Dutch, and/or Americans for necessary airlifting out of there. I was hoping that you were able to call the Embassy of the Netherlands in Chad, to let them know where you were.

What bothered me most this time was that you did not have the backup of a well-established group like MSF and IRC. And since the infrastructure of Africa Vision was just being started, you were wide open in terms of safety. Now you understand that when I went there, without the backup of any organization, the only crew I could rely on was the American Embassy. Not to adhere to their advice would have essentially been suicide.

Your brief e-mail notes helped in some way. At least we knew that you were alive and well, and doing your best. Your utmost.

Your mom and I have been in touch through Skype. Her inner strength and faith are admirable. I can only empathize with what your parents must feel. Yet your mom had an inner knowing that you would be okay. You already know that I made contact with folks there to make sure at least that people are looking out for you, though being with Gabriel's team certainly helps. I e-mailed the Dutch embassy and gave your name to them to make sure they know where you are right now. We can never take things for granted during unstable times like this. Situations can quickly reverse, even when one is feeling safe. After all, it is now a flat-out war over there.

The rebels seem determined this time to oust Chad's president, Idriss Déby. It seems that they are deliberately slowing down just to let the civilians and foreigners leave, as they don't want an international conflict. These are the news reports. Is this all about oil? And the almighty buck? About power?

About irrational territorialism? Insanity? All of the above?

One of the rebel group leaders is actually the president's nephew. The newspapers seem to believe that Sudan is backing up the Chadian rebels to overthrow President Déby. Sudan denies this. President Déby insists on staying in the palace, which is only about three minutes from the Hotel Meridien, and he refused to go when the French military offered to take him to safety. All in the news.

But it is hard to know what to believe in the news. News is all about perspectives and who owns the newspaper, I believe, though there are some excellent journalists and reporters out there who risk their lives to uplift the truth, the best they know how.

The most important thing is that you are alive and well, Dr. Buffalo. And that Gabriel and his team are all okay. It made my heart smile to see you all going inside the tank. However, that façade of security could not hide the fact that the rebels had anti-tank weapons. The news also reported that there were many dead bodies around the palace area in N'Djamena. And that the president was being guarded by some of his loyalists, though some are turning toward the rebels. In the news, John Prendergast talked about how the ousting of President Déby could imbalance the work that is being done regarding the Darfur refugees. The refugees are now truly in the midst of all of these. They don't need any more suffering. How much more can any human being take?

You are in my prayers and I'm sending you a loving white light all around you.

Dearest Dr. Buffalo,

Happy to know that you are okay in Gabon. What a tough thing to go through. But I had no doubt that you would be peaceful for some reason. Just remember always that you are loved by so many. And it is that Love that makes everything all right, no matter what happens. I wish I could give you, Gabriel, and the team there big hugs. Please give them all my love. God has been watching over you. There's so much more to learn and do. Just touch your forehead and then touch your heart. There I will be. You have my love.

Dearest Ashis,
Soul smiles. Great to hear from you today on Skype.
I "truth" you too, Dr. Buffalo.

And thank you for writing all your thoughts. I can visualize it all and feel it all. And I can see you smile. That inner peace kind of smile.

I can also feel your heart bleed for the Chadians, and sense your deep gratitude to God, the French military, Gabriel and his team, friends, and the people of Chad. And all of you who shared a bunker during this nightmare. You lived some moments there, Ashis. History truly starts in the Now. We all create and manifest history. Because each moment lived to the utmost is special, history does not have to repeat itself. Though I often wonder whether the thing that we call history may just be a spiritual flow that is timeless. History starts at this very moment.

You will be happy to know that your two favorite symbols, the eagle head that my brother Reggie carved, and the key to the city of Louisville … well, don't you worry. A little bird told me that they may miraculously appear and rise up like the phoenix.

Being in the midst of random shelling and bombing surely imbues in us compassion and empathy for soldiers everywhere in the world. Each fighting for their causes. Each fighting for what they believe in, whether we agree with it or not. There are many ways to be a soldier. We can be soldiers for peace. Soldiers for compassion and love.

My prayers are for all the Chadians, Africa, and the world. Africa is where our souls are; that's where we bring out the best in ourselves and others. It is there that the most vulnerable teach us about inner strength and courage. It is there that the neediest of all allow us to give our best compassion and love. It is there that we receive the best compassion and love. For they know the meaning of utmost pain, dignity, resilience.

Protection of Loved Ones

6 February 2008

Ashis dear,

"I'll take a bullet for you." That was the protective, reassuring, affectionate, and brotherly statement that Jun would say to us, always with that easy, familiar smile on his face. And we, his siblings, would say the same thing back to him. Yet it was so believable coming from Jun because he actually did take bullets (though with a bulletproof vest) to protect people he never knew. We could only hope to be able to do the same for him and others if the time ever arose.

His words came to my mind as I watched the StopGenocide-Now.org video, where all of you were dodging bullets. When all is said and done, it is probably quite instinctive to take a bullet for loved ones. No time to think. Just that protective instinct to become a shield of love. That shielding is best portrayed by a heroic man named Wesley Autrey in New York, who jumped down the subway tracks and covered and protected the body of another man who accidentally fell on the tracks. Utmost divine courage and compassion for the plight of another human being.

Last night Louisville was hit by a severe thunder- and windstorm. Many people died. I could hear ferocious, tornado-like sounds all around my house. I just kept on writing. It was another reminder that life can be taken away in a flash. More reason to keep focused on priorities in life. Sad to know that people died. And to realize that the families of the deceased are out there in anguish.

At a residential facility where I work, a place you visited when you were here, the teens anxiously told me that they had to huddle in the basement for protection in the middle of the night. Several of them were pretty scared by those strangely howling, powerful gusts of wind. All day the staff and I worked through their fear of dying from the tornado. It was a beautiful opportunity to positively reframe philosophies about life and death with the teens.

We addressed the issue of how bold they thought they were to risk their lives and risk destroying themselves for something so destructive as drugs and alcohol. Yet how ironic that they get scared to die from other reasons. In the depth of addiction, the so-called "twisted thinking" and basic loss of conscience can be gripping, baffling, dumbfounding. The craving and urge to use becomes more potent in their minds than their feelings for the people they genuinely love. The lying, stealing, apathy, and loss of loving ways become habits entrenched along with the addictions, leading people to further spirals of self-destruction.

Addictions can also be unhealthy attachments to people,

places, and things. Al-Anon addresses the issue of "detachment with love" in helping those who are codependent upon addicts. Those people believe that they love the addicts, but they often end up enabling the addictions because their denial compounds the convoluted layers of the addict's thinking.

However, after rehabilitation, many of our teens work on their recovery and become spiritually renewed. Instead of the twisted thinking, they go back to their basic values of inner peace, serenity, and love. There is nothing more beautiful to witness than the radiant faces of these teens softening and becoming more tender in the course of their recovery work. Their smiles come back. Their eye contact becomes more engaging. Gratitude and appreciation start to become the cornerstones of their everyday life.

But it's a daily trudge. One day at a time. One moment at a time, if need be. Self-construction through higher power rather than self-destruction. And then going beyond the humble innocence of the self.

The serenity prayer: "God, grant me the serenity to accept the things I cannot change, the courage to change the things I can, and the wisdom to know the difference." That prayer serves as the spiritual foundation of AA, NA, and their twelve step-programs. Meetings are ended by huddling together in a circle with arms around one another or holding hands, and saying this prayer together. By breaking down this prayer into parts, one gets to understand its profundity. And consequently, applying it to one's life is a stepping-stone to more hopefulness, joy, and a love for life. I love working with our teens, no matter how challenging any particular one may be. And I love our kids. During detoxification, they project a lot of inner bile toward the staff and me. Yet at the end of their treatment, the most important words created—"I love you" and "thank you"—are showered gently upon us. How can we not love these teens? They challenge my mind and heart to grow, professionally and personally, to the utmost.

Balancing the edge. When you write about that, I get this picture in my head of you either walking carefully on a tightrope, or balancing yourself at the edge of a balcony ledge of a tall building, or maybe even teeter-tottering at the edge of a cliff. Since there are no true guarantees in life except Love, well, it dawns on me that every moment is the edge. That in life we're constantly walking the edge and making choices as to what path to take. Yet most of the time, the edge is chosen for us, Ashis, as when we're compelled by a calling. And then it is like being blindfolded and "seeing beyond sight" as to what our life purpose and direction may be. Faith. That God will take care of all things. That there are higher reasons for all that happens. And as humans we know not the absolute answers to everything. That spirituality is that sweet surrender to the merging of all.

It is in our awareness of that oneness and love that our spirits flourish and grow.

The idea of embracing the moment brings out sublime thoughts. Free hugs for the moment. Wrapping ourselves around the Now and feeling every experience to the utmost, cherishing it, learning from it, and then teaching it to others, to bring out the best in all of us. Living life to its maximum. To its fullest. To its utmost.

The Call

11 February 2008

Dearest Ashis,

You must be resting and contemplating right now. And just being cloaked with the love and friendship of family and old, close friends. Many insights and perspectives float through my mind about all that happened in Chad, and just about life itself. *Mahasamadhi*—the final conscious abandonment of the physical body—can easily be seen as a merciless thief in the night. Yet physical death for many enlightened souls is no more than a dream. The transcendence to the spirit level, toward the heart of the Light. A theme of resurrection for others. Be meditation. Be still. Be Love.

It also occurred to me that destiny seems to place you right in the middle of manmade disasters, whereas I find myself in the midst of natural disasters. Did our souls just dive in the midst of this chaos? Amazing. With our deep affinity and love for people and Nature we manifest ourselves in the very core of what we passionately love. Where we can serve our utmost at full throttle. Many times, at the risk of it all. The call.

The Call

The shattered souls amidst the roaring flames
elucidate the hearts with dying ember
from searing pain and anguish,
hope that flickers
the rest of One immersed with love
to heal the chambers of abyss, oblivion
lasts, a moment in eternity.
In Love, be gone dualities,
The harmonies of life untapped;
The universal call
Explodes within one's core.
The sweltering, melting, dissolving
Fusion of Socratic wisdom and discernment
Where death begins, the rising of the Phoenix
Emerging from the ashes of despair to
Tantalize the myriad stars in heavenly skies
Behold! The light that comes from
nihil fiortor amore, *the dazzling imperfection*
Of humanity; exquisite fragrance of the
Spirits hover over forsaken sacred grounds;
The bells still toll for you and me
yet only in illusion,
Tumultuous fears and doubts, distractions from

The Call

the path
the transcendental yearnings of nomadic hearts
implore, the newness and the innocence of
journey unexplored; Ubuntu melodies that
linger floating misty moonlight mirth in beings;
a galaxy of hearts befuddled with the mysteries
of yonder aching for the merging of
the little One
with the Mighty All;
the tempest of tsunami
ocean wave encapsulated
in tiny glistening dewdrop gently captivated;
be aware, be still our hearts, be meditation
prayer of illumination from within;
where love is boundless, quantum vibrance
soar the soulful visions of compassion;
a destiny unscripted, sweet acceptance of a yearning
to be free from all; incarcerated freedom from
exquisite sampaguita beauty of feeling everything
where raindrops cascade like Nature's tears
where radiant sunsets, shimmering, glowing,
share the joyous inner knowing of a day well done
flowing, growing, sowing
when being is the catapult of
quintessential loving
and loving is the antidote for anecdotal fear
with gratitude sublime, elusive endless
echoes of tender past embraced
in Now lies the iridescent dawn of purpose
I learn there is no time, yet time is now

Utmost

Colossal wonderings of One life, One love
The living, the giving of being to UTMOST eternal
Ethereal longings feel the ardent air
To seek tabula rasa from
The Source.
Where Peace is home
Where Joy is play
Where Hope is dream
Where Bliss is smile
Where Light is laughter
Where Love is All.
Not even death
can stop The Call.

by Liz

Contemplation.
Inner Peace.

12 February 2008

Ashis dear,

Snow. Beautiful iridescent white snow. Lots of it. So I am stranded at home today and not able to go to work. Icy driveway and roads. Lots of branches across the yard. Contemplating the pristine nature blanketing my home and property gave me the spiritual stamina to keep shoveling. With white snow boots and triple-layered clothing, brown and matte gold Pashmina scarf wrapped around my head and neck, red gloves, and rusty old shovel in my hand, I thought about the thousands of people in China affected by the snowstorms. How do they do it? What must they be feeling at this time? Are people helping each other?

Here in Louisville, we have gone from tornadoes to blizzard. Yet people all take it in stride. It is tough for me to have to miss work as I know it would be extra work for other people, and patients are needing to be seen. Yet the icy layer on the driveway could dangerously slide even my Jeep into the busy street and into the ravine on the other side. The risks seem more than the benefits of going to work. My hope is that my patients stayed home today and didn't risk a trip into the office.

The beauty of snow melts my heart. Skiing has long been one of my favorite sports, almost to the point of addiction. Carving that soft gentle S as I ski down an undisturbed slope while seeing the panoramic beauty of the snowcapped mountains surrounding a lake—that always leaves me inspired. Breathtaking. Heavenly in Tahoe. Deer Valley in Utah. Whistler in British Colombia. Lovely memories with family and inner circle of friends.

However, last night, as the snow was falling unstoppably in the metro Louisville area, it took me two hours to drive from work downtown to the east end, which is normally a half-hour drive. People were cautious, and that was good. A lady ahead of me got stuck. As she attempted to turn on to the expressway, her car went sideways. I stopped and checked to see if she was okay. She said she was just a bit stunned. Her cell phone proved to be a great security tool as she called her family to come and help her out. We made sure that her car was situated in a way that it did not obstruct traffic. She did not hit her head or get physically hurt, and was lucid and alert.

Meanwhile, the snow kept falling and people were honking their horns impatiently. She said for me not to worry; her family would be there soon. Just in case, I gave her my cell phone number and asked for hers. I checked to make sure that her cell phone battery was not low. It was fully charged. Safety and communications. They go hand in hand.

Later, I called her and learned that she was on her way home, though they had to leave her car right where it had gotten stuck.

Marissa, David, and I spent the night talking about life and philosophies that have shaped us in some way. Many interesting insights about interpersonal dynamics. We laughed at the complexities and simplicities of life. And we were serious about the needs of the Ugandan Women for Empowerment through Crafts (UWEC), and their devotion and dedication in their artistry to help each other. Marissa has done a wonderful job in supporting and encouraging Rosette, the founder of UWEC. The two of them have become soul sisters and they communicate almost daily about ways to uplift their cause and mission. The idea is to work together with utmost respect, harmony, and love while caring for one another to succeed.

It was disorienting to drive back to my house in the middle of the night through so much snow. Though driving at a snail's pace, and with rapt attention, I nevertheless found myself driving for a moment on someone's front yard. The street definitions were completely blurred out by the snow blanket.

I've had a Jeep for fifteen years, and it has been the best advice I ever got from my dad. I always wondered why he loved driving Jeeps, even though he had a penchant for fast cars. My windshield wipers and car heaters were working at maximum and I focused intensely on the road. Only after I got to the main road did I start composing a song in my mind about Free Hugs, in preparation for a campaign friends and I plan to do in Aruba.

The tranquility of an isolated beach. The sparkling peace of the turquoise sea. The cuddling warmth of the sun. Those images consoled me as I continued to drive the narrow, winding roads to my house. Ever since I started doing missions and relief work more intensively, it has been a long time since I truly had an island vacation. My Jeep was unable to go uphill on my driveway. It kept slipping backwards, which was a bit hairy because of the ravine across the street. Heels and all, I left it at the bottom of the hill and stomped through the thick layer of virgin snow all across my front yard and driveway. Peace. Looking around, I took a deep breath and felt utmost serenity.

Some reflections:

A few days ago, a caring, nurturing adoptive parent came in with a calmer, more peaceful look on his face than he'd had before. A ten-year old boy appeared to be in the same space as the parent this time. I could tell that the session would be a very positive one. Their faces always tell the stories faster than their words. Their gestures and beaming smiles openly give way to describing the inner joy both felt at the boy's progress in his treatment. This boy had been abused physically and sexually by a relative and he had eventually been taken out of his home. His parents were chemically dependent and the boy had witnessed domestic violence several times. He suffered nightmares and his school grades dropped.

Ashis, when I first saw this boy he looked like he was shell-shocked. He had bags around his eyes. His appetite was poor.

When he was placed under the consistent guidance of the foster parents who eventually became his adoptive parents, he improved significantly—with the added help of therapy and a low-dose antidepressant.

The main residual problem was that the boy tended to steal,

and to lie to his family. These behaviors made him more alienated as other kids started not to trust him. His parents worked very hard at positively reinforcing him when he was truthful. During the previous session, I told him that I was glad about something. That he was not very good at lying anymore because people tended to know that he was not being honest. And I added that by now he probably was much better at being honest than being dishonest, so why not give full-time honesty a try. That honesty meant that he is also willing to accept the consequences of not telling the truth. And that with honesty he will be able to preserve his self-respect and self-esteem.

Lying tends to make us all lose ourselves because, after a while, the shackles of lies we have laid upon ourselves block our connection to who we really are.

Long story short, I challenged and double-dared the boy to be honest, and to have the courage to do so. Something must have clicked. In this most recent session, the adoptive father said that he has done much better.

The boy was all smiles. He was getting along better with others. His grades were improving and that is a biggie for him.

What makes some people honest and what makes others tell untruths? Honesty is known to be the foundation of spiritual recovery. There is nothing more moving than when a recovering addict does his or her fourth and fifth steps. Doing a fourth step of taking a moral inventory of the wrongs they have done can be a daunting experience. It leaves people naked. Vulnerable. Defenseless.

We keep a close eye on the teens when they are doing this step, as it tends to reveal many things that the teen had previously been lying about. And it brings to the surface experiences that the teen had been repressing and wanting to completely forget because of perceived pain. Sometimes, as they do their fourth step they feel the flashbacks of the original pain. Yet as they do their fifth step, sharing their honest life experiences with a trusted person like a chaplain, a sponsor, or a minister, something beautiful happens. The restless agitation gives rise to an inner peace that shows in the teens' facial expressions and actions. Something profound happens. Like a clean slate for the soul. Back to innocence. Back to joy. Back to acceptance of self. Back to truth. Back to love.

Ashis, many times I have thought that the honest, innocent, clean mental slate of a child is what many of us seek every day. Children and adults with post-traumatic stress end up having vivid flashbacks and have difficulties ridding their minds of all the chaotic trauma they have experienced. As I write this, my mind goes back to the victims of multi-torture. Many of the refugees we treat here in Louisville have suffered atrocities. Each one of them deals with those intense memories differently. Many have difficulty talking about what they've gone through, perhaps feeling that being honest about those feelings and memories may reactivate even further their old pain. Others are able to sublimate and keep themselves busy with constructive activities.

13 February 2008, Wee hours of the morning

Dearest Ashis,

I am so sorry about your uncle. He waited for you before he passed on. Mahasamadhi. My deepest condolences to you and your family. Please give your parents and your extended family my hugs. Wish I was there to console your family, just like you did with all of us when my brother passed away.

It was great to talk to your mom today and extend my prayers and thoughts to your family. I'm hoping that she can visit here in Louisville. It would be fun to garden together and just smell the roses and jasmine. Your dad said that he used to have work here in Louisville. How amazing is that?

My bags are almost packed. No doubt I will be sleeping in the plane. Aruba, here I come. To relax and decompress. Will and his friends are organizing the Free Hugs campaign, so that will be a great gateway to raising awareness about our causes: clean water for the world and refugees. There must be a reason why I need to be in Aruba. Wish you could have joined us. Islands are my fantasy places. The more remote and exotic, the better.

Looking forward to seeing you again soon. Pray for me, please. If I start talking like I just want to stay in Aruba forever and lie around on a hammock with flowers on my hair and sell pukka shells, well, you are my mission partner. Just wake me up and remind me gently, even firmly, of what we have to do. We all have our weaknesses. Let us help each other away from distractions. There is a lot to do for the people suffering.

I've started work on creating a nonprofit organization, which will be called Phoenix Global Humanitarian Foundation. Mission? To serve those who are suffering from disasters, tragedies, and losses, with love and compassion. Our African mission projects are all within that mission.

Relaxing for a few days should help me maintain a sense of inner peace. And I will be more replenished and prepared to mobilize people to the Uganda international conference "Healthy and

Safe Water for the World" in July, in Mubende. Time for me to rest a little bit before going to the airport, and to hope I can successfully get out of my snow-covered driveway. And I am off, Dr. Buffalo … Hugs to you.

Hiatus

13 April 2008

Back from writing hiatus. Many distractions. The take-it-easy attitude of the Aruban islanders permeated throughout me. Much needed. I had a blast! Will was an excellent host and the Free Hugs Aruba was a great way to uplift the clean water for the world cause. Now the video is on YouTube.

Contemplating the turquoise waters, the pristine beaches, the mellow sunsets gave me a sense of deep inner peace, Ashis. A slower pace allows for more meditative moments and leads to more peaceful perspectives about life. What is truly important. Priorities. There is something special about friendships that thrive on making good things happen in our world.

Ashis, I am still reeling from having video-witnessed you, Gabriel, and the StopGenocideNow crew almost get killed out there in N'Djamena. After watching the SGN website video of all of you in such danger, it gave me a jolt, a sense of vulnerability about the things that can so easily happen in humanitarian work. Many times, we become desensitized to the dangers, and find it easy to justify why we're going someplace where we could become part of the cold statistics of mortality. Something in me just wanted to escape and run away. With my brother Jun's death, and with you almost getting killed out there, it became overwhelming. And I had to get a distance. And I had to re-understand again why we are doing what we are doing. I had to overcome an emotional short circuit. That you were continuing to write your part of *Utmost*, and calmly Holosync meditating, while the mortars, bombs, and bullets were flying all over the place, is something hard to grasp. But I know that writing and meditating keep you peaceful. I certainly am the same way.

Yet after all that bedlam, we both somehow stopped writing. Perhaps we needed to take a break, to let our thoughts and emotions become fertile ground so we can convey many of the important things we have learned during the last couple of years.

Grief about Jun's death brought my momentum in intensive short-term global missions to a halt. A couple of missions had to be canceled; one of them was the Hands On Disaster relief work in Peru. The earthquake there demolished so much and affected so many families and children. I will still find a way to go there and follow up. I also want to follow up with Pakistan and their earthquake relief. One of my friends who works with a humanitarian organization lost three close friends and their families in that huge earthquake.

Before that disaster he worked as an accountant for one of

the big four international firms; now he's back in the for-profit world.

Pakistan is mostly Muslims, of course, and it is truly tough to hear Pakistani friends feel the pain of being stereotyped as terrorists. Going through security in airports must be hellacious. The vilification of certain religions by political leaders, in their desire to be endorsed by the majority religion, can truly lead to continued wars, hatred, and divisiveness in our world.

Many times, we tend to project to others what we believe may be "bad" about us. Then the split of "good" and "bad" happens once again, creating a disharmony between people of various religions.

I am happy that platforms like Facebook are starting to give credence to the idea of a boundary-less world. How can people truly stay within the bounds of their own countries when through the Internet they have created friendships all over the world? The very positive side of technology leads us to creating a cozier, more reachable world, based on the Web and other amazing communications tools like Skype and Yahoo. Relationships are now happening via these technologies and people are reaching out across the miles to connect with one another. I know of a spirited humanitarian man and woman from different parts of the world who have decided to get married this month, before they have even met each other face-to-face. Love knows no boundaries. And love can be creative and courageous. I wish them both all the happiness in the world.

The last few months of writing hiatus has been an incredible learning experience for me. I have communicated with people across the world, talking about their lives, relationships, families, friends, work, dreams. For many, humanitarianism has led us to transcend cultural, socioeconomic, academic, religious, and psychological boundaries. Though more destigmatization is necessary, the sexuality of being gay and/or bisexual is now more open in many parts of the world. In cultures that are more repressed in sexuality, taboos are being challenged stealthily, and many times openly. The world is changing indeed. And the lesser the boundaries, the more the love. And the only semipermeable boundaries maintained are those that protect people from harm. I don't truly know what the answers are, as always.

Meeting new people across the world, we start to grow even more. The constant exchange of ideas helps dissolve boundaries. Even with music. As I have always loved the Beatles and have been painstakingly learning the Blackbird riff, I am learning to enjoy Ben Harper's soulful songs like "Morning Yearning," "Forever," "A Better Way," and "Waiting on an Angel." And Leona Lewis's rendition of "Here I Am" is moving. Andrea Bocelli and Josh Groban have been endowed with breath-stopping voices. Music has a way of universalizing everything we think about at the time we are listening to it. Each beautiful melody, depending on how we feel, becomes an unforgettable utmost experience.

Perspective

21 April 2008

Tempest. Passions swirling in my soul. Somehow, my inner spirit feels wide open, almost with a need to slowly close up. There has to be balance somehow. Or maybe not. My heart seems like a vulnerable and gaping wound, so sensitive and raw for what is coming my way. And lots of unforeseen experiences are indeed coming my way. Truth be told, Ashis, I see it all again as a child, delighted with every gentle, translucent, ephemeral bubble coming toward me while we danced at the "Hearts Coming Together" event in Canton, Ohio.

I am not quite sure what to make of some of my recent experiences with people. I've experienced some fascinating connections. Beautiful, enchanting, disarming connections. And some feel like IV heroin. (And I've never even had heroin, nor do I intend to experiment.) My not writing so much over the last few months has given me a chance to more deeply feel the essence of friendships and relationships with people. They feel like learning experiences that through the passage of time can become the foundation for positive changes in our lives.

You make me laugh out loud, Booff! Your responses to all my mischief crack me up. Probably much like my responses to your mischief. So now here you are trying your best to take it easy. And now here I am embracing the world with abandon, accepting come what may. Going with the Flow, I say. I need my rest, you say. And hopefully you will have the season respite and retreat in South America.

Yet you say that there is still this deep attraction for what is on the edge. The lure of the utmost.

My flight connections from Louisville to Canton, Ohio, for the Hearts Conference were a series of divine disconnections. Bumped. Waited. Standby. And meeting several people in the Chicago airport—talking to them, as usual, about clean water for the world and about Darfur refugees made the delay worthwhile. Seeing you, John, and John's mom, Cynde, in the Akron/Canton airport made me happy. Happy enough to play wheelchair-racing in the airport with another couple while waiting for my luggage. Remember when we saw a couple on wheelchairs? We thought they actually were wheelchair-bound and decided to hang out with them and play with them. Much laughter.

As much as I love Louisville and New York City, I also love Canton. The people have always welcomed us there. Our dancing in the Canton fountains symbolically represents the daily freshness of our missions and causes. The city represents America's grassroots. And I love the sunsets in Perception Park. Just like the sunsets in Uganda. But more, I love the people.

28 April 2008, Chicago

Dear Dr. Gazelle,

It has been a while since I have taken time to sit down and taken time to write. Traveling to all nooks and corners of the USA has been great. A plethora of meetings with new friends, old friends, people of all ages and backgrounds. In just two months I have been to over fifteen states and at least forty different regions. Months of intense travel, storytelling, and interacting with middle schools, high schools, universities, church groups, activists, and humanitarian workers.

One thing is common: all over the USA I have been received like a prince. People have taken me into their houses, fed me, and power-washed the dirt of the road off me. I have been pampered, and that is the only way this grueling schedule of some fifty talks could be a success.

I have learned a lot, and one of the key things has been realizing that being a one-man show leads you to burn fast. A team is needed to support all the potential initiatives in my mind. Many people in different fields are interested in helping out for a good cause. Stepping up to be the change to make this world a better place.

Another thing I've learned is that at all levels of the USA there is an opportunity to reframe the negative paradigm that seems to be attached to Africa. Over the last twenty-five presentations, I mainly used a slide-show PowerPoint presentation which had about three hundred photos. Roughly 225 are positive, with radiantly beautiful children and adults in day-to-day life; twenty-five are about violence, and fifty about illness.

In my mind I see the laughs and the opportunities in Africa despite ongoing horrific events like the genocide in Darfur. That is the message I have been trying to deliver to the audiences. It seems to resonate. There is an open mind to the potential that even the most downtrodden refugees are in fact in another state of mind, and have the ultimate potential for human growth.

When you lose all is when you have it all.

Every single time I see the photos, it inspires me to look at what is possible. To think about what I can do to make an impact. To ponder how I can get many groups behind me to help out those in Africa who are in some ways less fortunate than we are. I believe the photos, combined with stories from real life, give people ample opportunity to reflect, to care, to open their hearts, to start learning, to unite, and to use their talents and skills to make a difference!

All steps, even baby steps, in the right direction will lead to a kinder, more inclusive world. In my mind, part of the misfortune of so many people in the world is not due to lack of compassion, but a simple lack of knowledge. Hearing and seeing the voices from Darfur makes people step up.

As my tour progressed, I got more and more tired. Doing your own finance, logistics, and travel arrangements makes you forget that in fact you are out there to connect with people. Next time, I am sure, a team of people will help me out in the fields I am not so good at.

Back to the moment! A golden opportunity landed in my lap. The Sudanese People's Liberation Movement (SPLM) has a conference in Juba, Sudan, planned around May 7–17, 2008. From at least two sides I will get help. An official invitation to the conference may be arranged, and the finance to travel has been kindly offered by a caring individual. I shall go to Juba in about ten days for two weeks and I am very excited about it. It gives me a prime opportunity to meet up with people working at the Ministry of Health, the Teaching Hospital, the local clinics, the politicians, the movers and the shakers, but mostly the local Dinka, Nuer, Shilluk, and the other at least fifty tribes from southern Sudan.

Recently, I have met a bright young Lost Boy named Jacob. He is a pre-med student and has the ambition and dream to build a health clinic in his home village, Maar. There are moments in life when you know that the combination of talent, perseverance, and focus will lead to a not-so-easy objective being reached. I have a very strong hunch that this clinic will be up and running in only a few years. His village is two days' walk from Bor, which in turn is a three-hour drive from Juba.

A snapshot of American history in the making. Obama's path crossed mine in Pittsburgh. This natural powerhouse spoke from the heart, bringing memories of JFK's strong words: Ask not what your country can do for you but what you can do for your country.

He talked about how all of us are here to serve this world to become a better place. Of all the applause he drew that night, those words drew the deepest and most resonating of responses.

There is this moment—the moment of now—where the world can shift paradigm. Away from "me, me, me" to "us, us, us." From an exclusive society to an inclusive one. From a destructive culture to a building one. Be the potential that we all have within.

Divergent Focus

Be the Poet
The Clown
The Doctor
The Thinker
The Doer
The Inspirer
The Inspired
The Teacher
The Student
and
remain always The Child
Dreams are just blueprints in Mind
Of reality to be created
Impossible is not a Word
Reframe it to a "do" and "able"
In the Playground of this Mind
Obstacles are Opportunities
Stumbling blocks are Steps Up
To Realization
Of the Whole
Smiling, radiating One
The Sun's Ray tickles my Skin
Focused UV AB
With a Prism

The rainbow's Focus Divergent
Of One
Multitude
Divergent Focus
Embracing ambiguity
One is All
All is One.

by Ashis

16 May 2008

Dearest Liz,

As a transition to the next step, here are some highlights from the conference of the Sudanese People's Liberation Movement.

Being free.

A long line of men speak.

In the air it is clear that egos arise.

To clash for power.

Yet it is in such a democratic arena that you would hope struggle for a new Sudan will come.

Only if the division does not overcome

And the Unity overcomes.

I have chosen another country.

There has to be a stability in where you work.

To perform and to be.

Peace helps out a lot.

I will be working in Sudan but the storybook on Chad will be temporarily on the shelf. Chad is in my heart, but too troubled to be addressed immediately. The rebel/freedom fighters' attack on N'Djamena at the end of January 2008 was one in a string of attacks. And it seems that the current regime at one point will crumble. Not the place to construct therefore.

At the convention here, it seems there is that vibe for peace, the hope for reconstruction. That being the case, it is here where my wings will stop beating for a while and a temporary nest may be built. I am here to review some of the issues we have raised in writing *Utmost*, and to ponder how much we have answered them, so the book can end with at least an attempt to define or demonstrate what the utmost is.

Inexorable Mission

1 June 2008

Dearest Ashis,

Inexorable. You and I were laughing about that word because the author of a book we both read kept on using it repeatedly. Relentless. Unstoppable. Perhaps that word caught our eye because it is an adjective for the way we focus on our missions. Does relentlessness in actualizing our life purpose mean the utmost?

Ashis, though you were very exhausted from all your talks around the USA, it was meaningful to have some rest time with you in Houston, New York City, Canton, and Louisville. I appreciate meeting Babu and Juno, your cousins in Houston who opened their home to me. And their children Rohina and Rohak are adorable. Little Rohak's charming Jim Morrison-like impish smile can disarm anyone who even tries to discipline him. And

New York City just seems to be our city, Booff. I just can't believe all the hours we spent tirelessly walking around the Soho-Tribeca area in the cold. Talking about everything. Discussing the sensitive issues regarding China and Tibet, and how it all impacts Sudan as well. Brrrr ... yet how heartwarming to know that in one of the restaurants where we wolfed down three tiers of seafood, we by coincidence found out that the owner had held a fundraising event for Darfur.

Speaking with that restaurant owner made us realize there are people out there who care. That made the food all the more appetizing for us, didn't it, Booff? Yet it seems like such a contradiction to dine so wonderfully while discussing Sudan, where the refugees so often starve. Then, the contrarians that we both are, we decided to watch some random movies. Two of them back to back. Rather than see plays in NYC, we see movies. Okay, then. So, to our own amazement, we bought the biggest bucket of popcorn and enjoyed two perfectly different kinds of movies. Lots of laughter and exchange of irreverent wit, as always.

And of course, we danced our hearts out in Canton and had fun with friends there. The Fieldcrest, where the Hearts Coming Together group hung out, was just lovely. The landscape, the bedroom suites, and the lodge are simply beautiful and so conducive to group meetings and retreats. At the conference it was great to have Will there via Web from Aruba, joining the open space discussions. I had to leave a day ahead as I had to go immediately back to work. You stayed over at Jamil's home, which he kindly opened to you.

You came here to Louisville twice. The first time, oh my gosh! We got all decked out in fancy white clothes to attend your first Kentucky Derby. Thanks to my brother-in-law, Brian, we came up with good tickets at the last minute. We spent time shopping for your attire, and just played around in the malls like teenagers.

I hardly ever shop in malls anymore, so it felt like a novelty to me as well. And then we stopped by a toy store. There we saw what was perfect for you and your head! A gold and black pharaoh hat. Amazingly, it fit your head just as well as well it did as your persona. A kingly imago.

I wore my gold Lady Luck sunglasses with horseshoe designs. The Derby gave us more attention than anyone could ever want to have in a lifetime. Especially you. People were so enamored with your pharaoh hat that they were calling you King Tut, Ramsis … and bowing to honor you. Everywhere we walked, they bowed to you, and you played your regal role well. I could not stop laughing so hard. You in your white suit and matte gold shirt and pharaoh hat. And me in my frilly lace dress and white hat.

When we stood around the common area during intermissions, people began taking our photographs like crazy. At one point, a very drunken woman asked you to take a photo with her and then suddenly grabbed one of your hands and put it on her breast. You looked at me like, "I didn't do anything." I feel a pang of sadness when I imagine when those who suffer from alcoholic intoxication or blackouts realize what they have done. Being sober and free from toxins allows us to live life more to the utmost, for we remember our experiences more clearly.

It is all play, Ashis. That seems to happen when you and I get together. It just happens. Our chemistry compels us to play to the utmost. People may be tempted to judge us harshly to "grow up" when they see us just turn the world into a loving playground. And some have. And there are times when I have to pull back a bit for perspective. And I come out with this.

Our mission and work are so deeply adult because of their responsibilities that our souls balance us out by calling the child within us to come out and play. In the harshness of what we see and experience in our jobs, in the depth of responsibilities in ensuring that people are kept alive and thriving after physical, emotional, and psychological sufferings, our childlike natures bring us back to the innocence of love and life. A clean slate. A sacred place where we remember to live to the utmost and to be.

And with the tenderness and compassion for ourselves that we assimilate within, we are able to give more to those who suffer.

We both have so many families and friends who love us, Ashis. I am so grateful for that. Therein lies the sense of abundance we have in our spirits to give more to those who lack the sense of love and care in their lives. Perhaps we are able to give our utmost each day because we are so cognizant of all the unconditional love from our families and friends. We couldn't give it if we didn't already have it. And in our case, we realize that we give what we have so much of, pouring it out there where it is most needed. In sporadic times of fatigue, self-pity, and ingratitude, we sometimes fall short of that grateful realization. Yet, I think, we bounce back quickly, especially when there is a call or need.

Speaking of calls, with the earthquake in China and Cyclone Nargis in Myanmar, it hurts not to be able to go there. One good thing is that China has called out for psychiatrists around the world to help out the children suffering from acute stress from their losses. Myanmar's leaders are cautious and guarded about having the humanitarian community help them, though they have now allowed a certain number of relief workers from very select international relief organizations.

One thing that concerns me in just about every disaster is

governmental lack of awareness of the need of outside help from the very beginning. Even though there are many competent local relief workers where the disaster happens, many of them are already deeply affected by the situation, barely able to respond to the needs of others, no matter how much they may want to.

This requires a more objective group of relief workers, from the outside, to help out. Many of the local relief workers are already hit by acute stress, having lost family and or friends.

Stacy, Heather, Alex, and I have just formed and cofounded the LIGHT team: Louisville Local and International Grassroots Humanitarian Team. We will meet again after Heather and Alex get married on June 7, to solidify the name and the plans. The name gives us an opportunity to help mobilize other humanitarians in various cities around the world, to help them jumpstart their own humanitarian teams. We all like the acronym LIGHT so we now have a team e-mail: Lightforhope@gmail.com. So if we ultimately choose that name, we can have Louisville LIGHT spreading to Indianapolis LIGHT, to Canton LIGHT, etc., adding each new city's name to the key word, LIGHT.

LIGHT is the sparkplug team that will champion the mission of The Phoenix Global Humanitarian Foundation. PGHF's mission is to serve those who suffer disaster, losses, and tragedies. LIGHT is the link between uplifting awareness for the local grassroots humanitarian needs and mobilizing education about the global needs. The idea again is ensuring the integration of local and global awareness.

PGHF will soon acquire its 501c3 status, to be able to continue the work of caring for the needs of refugees, those who suffer from contaminated water, those who suffer from mental illness and chemical dependency, those who are incarcerated and marginalized because of AIDS, like the orphaned children of AIDS, the most suffering of the poorest of the poor.

I believe in collaborations. I also would like to start a project to serve the Lakota Native Americans in South Dakota. Marissa and Jackie have already started doing something for both Pine Ridge reservations and Rosebud. The Lakotas are known for their incredibly profound sense of spirituality. Their culture focuses on keeping things simple: being simple, being calm, and walking in prayer and beauty. I can certainly learn a lot from spending time with people with sacred spirituality, and hopefully I can be helpful to them, too.

Together, we are all much smarter and more creative than just one of us alone. The concept of aggregate wisdom. I am now in the process of searching for a board of directors who are impassioned about service to others on a local and global level. My sister Marissa is working on a logo and website for PGHF. The moment I made a decision to start this NPO, my heart felt relieved. So I know that we can serve others a lot out there, especially after acquiring a 501c3, which, as you know, allows people to list their contributions to the charity for tax deductions.

Another project I want to start is writing children's books about disaster and how to cope. I want to make them applicable to various cultures, and all types of disasters. It can easily be a series, and most of all the books will be helpful in facilitating the healing process for children affected by disasters in many parts of the world. My training in child psychiatry and my experiences with disaster relief work make it very compelling for me to write these books hoping it can help many. I already have a title: *One Day … Something Happened.* Each book would be subtitled with whatever type of disaster is in the story, whether it's an earthquake, a hurricane, or a volcanic eruption. And for the manmade disasters, a subtitle can be, *I Was Called a Refugee*, or *There Was a War*.

Lately I have been helping mobilize the Healthy and Safe Water for the World International Conference in Mubende, Uganda on July 8–11, 2008. The LIGHT team will be flying together to Entebbe before the eighth, and will have a short stopover in Dubai. The Rural Health Care Foundation (RHCF), under the medical leadership of Dr. Dickson Ssenoga, will be the host.

Having the grassroots organization in Mubende take the leadership role in an international conference is a statement in itself. The idea is to encourage and empower a dedicated grassroots organization to lead others in serving the welfare of their community by creating a mega-voice about the global problem of contaminated water in our world.

Facebook has been a helpful means of gathering people from various parts of the world to go. We are hoping to help set up a McGuire water purifier there, and the LIGHT team will get trained at New Life in Underwood, Indiana. There are already more than one hundred McGuire water purifiers in Myanmar.

Ashis, you met the LIGHT team and you felt their enthusiasm and desire to serve when you were here. Interestingly, the day you met them was also the day we met Dylan Wilk of Gawad Kalinga. Gawad Kalinga is a nonprofit organization founded in the Philippines. He focuses on creating healthy communities by building houses, ensuring health care and clean water, educating people with value formation and basic health practices in the created village.

Dylan is a self-made man from the UK who was blown away when he learned about what Gawad Kalinga (GK) was doing in the Philippines. Essentially, Dylan found his life purpose there—

Utmost

all the more so after he fell in love with the GK's founder's daughter and they became husband and wife. A beautiful love story based on humanitarianism.

Interestingly, GK just got started in South Africa, only a week before we met Dylan. So you and I talked to Dylan about how GK concepts might also be applied to Sudan.

The issue of value formation is vital. Though social entrepreneurism has become a global mantra because of the innovative ideas of Mohammed Yunus, the economics Nobel Prize winner from India, there are places—especially in Africa—where it may not work as well. My thoughts lead more to integrating both humanitarian-charity activities and social entrepreneurism. I think people need both. Again, it's not an either/or choice.

Ashis, I missed you when we were doing the very first Free Hugs campaign here in Louisville. Our mayor, Jerry Abramson, was supportive of LIGHT and came by to give us all hugs. That was the same day of his bike and hike healthy Louisville project, which I totally support. I still remember our first Free Hugs campaign in New York City, which we have yet to put on YouTube.

Last night as we were Skyping, it dawned on both of us how much we have learned about all the cutting-edge technology of internet social platforms. Facebook, Twitter, Flock, YouTube, and Seesmic have all taken up a lot of our time, yet we are learning so much. I particularly enjoy Seesmic and its community. There is something about seeing people's faces and learning their nuances, their facial expressions, their reactions. Though some can be good actors and create personas in Seesmic, I still feel more comfortable seeing people's faces rather than just reading people's blogs without knowing the people behind the writings. When someone posts in Seesmic, it is clear that at least we know who they are, whether they decide to troll or to be positive participants in this video community.

Though Seesmic is still in its alpha testing, I think it is a very promising social platform. It has been great to have video communications, even if only briefly, with people like Deepak Chopra, and to be able to be in the same thread as Paulo Coelho. Yesterday, I had a gardening and Seesmic day because I had to get my Jeep's window fixed and I had no transportation all day. I am even learning about CamTwist and how to connect YouTubes in Seesmic and upload photos from my desktop through CamTwist. All this information technology is exciting for me.

So, Ashis. How are you doing today, Booff? I am happy to know that you are able to relax in Mexico and that you've met a man who is something of a guru for you there. He teaches you about focus and humility. I believe that focus is about integrating and converging everything—all our skill sets, all we've learned— all into one process, rather than just focusing on one subject or topic. And when we start seeing the humility in others, that marks the point in our lives when we start recognizing our own humility.

I believe focus and humility are already within us. We just need to be aware that they are there, and that we want to be in touch with them.

I remember our heart-to-heart in my front yard, Ashis. Sacred space. Right on the bench under a tree. It ended up with you and me lying on our stomachs on the grass while Seesmic-ing about Love and Truth in a joking manner. We sang "All You Need Is Love," except you substituted the word "truth" for love. Though we both agreed that we need both Love and Truth.

Funny. We can be so absurd together, Booff. I like it. Being with you has allowed me to cut through all the boundaries people squabble over—race, creed, age, gender, lifestyles. Many times, we do and say things to almost back each other off when we feel too close. Yet, the reality is that we already accept that our souls are connected. We have grown to accept each other with so much friendship, laughter, and love. I have shared many things with you that would have overloaded another person's psyche. Yet because of the richness of our experiences in living life to the utmost day by day, you are able to handle what I dish out. And you know that I understand you, and can handle your quirks, as you handle mine.

We struggle with doing the spiritual alone or with someone we love when in truth, we can be alone and be with who we love all at the same time. I remember once reading that the ability to embrace ambiguity was a trait that Leonardo da Vinci had, and so have many others through history with great minds and evolved thinking. I believe that it all has to do with the and/and rather than either/or principle. The faster we are at seeing the and/and, the more we grow and feel the interconnectedness in our world. Someone also said, and I am paraphrasing, that for every truth, the opposite truth is equally true. Interesting thought. Interesting truth.

As you can see, we are close to the end of our book, Ashis.

As you said before, this book is our emotional bond. A spiritual baby. For it contains intricate intimate pieces of our hearts and souls, looking to be born. To offer some of our humble Light and Love to the world. Our utmost. Dr. Buffalo and Dr. Gazelle. Remind me to thank God for you. And remind me to thank you just for you.

Mexico City, Friday, 6 June 2008

Dear Dr. Gazelle,

In the Ramayana, there is a giant named Khumbakarna. When he is not used in warfare he sleeps and sleeps for months on end. Before he goes to war he eats for days on end. I think I may have learned how Khumbakarna feels.

You are so right. I was exhausted in the USA. All the talks and travel are like a source of energy, yet organizing it all drains me. At moments I have longed to be Khumbakarna. In the back of my mind had been thoughts of a break in humanitarian work for several months, to truly recharge. It seems inconceivable to give your utmost when your battery is empty.

And so instead of running from party to party here in Mexico City, I have been sleeping, sleeping, and sleeping. Eating home-cooked food and being pampered in a family setting. Seeing Harry Potter movies (numbers 3, 4, and 5) and *Pan's Labyrinth*. And then yesterday, this thought came to me more or less out of the blue, right after my friend Evonne asked me the question: "What are you looking forward to?"

My deep-felt answer was Being! Each moment. Losing wishes, dreams, demands, anxiety, stress, fear, and other emotions. Just being in the moment. A moment where you can feel love for the world. Looking back, it is possible to recognize where all that positivity has come from. First you had sent about twelve pages of *Utmost*. It is always a joy to read where we are going with our firstborn.

To digress a bit, this whole dialogue that we've undertaken

in writing the book has been an eye-opener, a soul-twister, a ride on the roller coaster, and always an ultimate joy. Slowly learning to shed all the layers and writing it straight—that has been fun. Secondly, I had returned from a historical moment in Sudanese history: the second Sudanese People's Liberation Movement National Conference.

It feels as if true effort is being made to wrest the Sudan in a democratic method from the current dictators, and it was brilliant to attend. In the process, people from all twenty-five states of the Sudan came together to deliberate for leadership in the party, a constitution, a strategy for the elections, and a strategy for leadership for the country.

Sudan has suffered way too long. After they finally achieved independence in 1956, they have faced civil war for over thirty-nine years. It is time for peace. The bullies in Khartoum are doing everything in their power to derail the process, of course, with the sad climax the destruction of the village Abyei. A home for twenty-six thousand Dinka tribespeople no longer exists, and a larger group of about ninety-five thousand was sent on the run by the Sudanese Armed Forces. Why? There is oil in the ground!

Despite this ultimate slight, the Southern Sudanese did not go for all out war and are hoping and planning to defeat the National Congress Party in fair and square elections in Sudan.

Utmost, in my mind, can mean having the heart not to respond with violence to provocations of the nature of the slaughter in Abyei. History will judge that regime responsible for it harshly, and as if to prove my point, the International Criminal Court is now prosecuting the entire Sudanese government for their obvious policies and involvement to destroy Darfur.

Wishes

Vera Cruz, 9 June 2008

Dear Dr. Gazelle,

Believe it or not, The Beatles "Ob La Di Ob La Da" is blaring in my ears. It has been three joyous days here. I have been near-adopted by a Mexican family, the family of Dr. Pilli, a dear friend of my friend Caesar. A neighbor's wedding led to utmost joy. Dancing and eating in the streaming rain in front of the house of the newlyweds. The original plan was to travel as fast as possible to Playa del Carmen, but playing it day by day is great.

Liz, if there is one thing I am working on, it is to let things be. Whatever you truly wish will come to you.

The Journey

Vera Cruz-Playa del Carmen, 10 June 2008

Another day, another journey. You know I love to travel, perhaps because of some gypsy blood mixed into my Indian and Dutch genes? Being in motion makes the words flow easily as well. As we are nearing the end of this epistle, I would like to look back and then forward.

When we started this book we joked that it would be a three hundred-page tome about our experiences, feelings, and thoughts. As the book then progressed I felt more and more relaxed about unpeeling the layers. Nothing to show but bare nakedness. The title of the book—*Utmost*—was the step in life that represented well my state of mind, and I think yours as well, as we recalled our life-changing experiences of 2007 and 2008. An intense passage for both us. For a plethora of reasons: your losses of dear and near

(Mom and brother Jun), my confrontations with violence, robberies, attacks, aerial bombardments, and an evacuation. My uncle's death in India. Your plans for early retirement while starting up the Phoenix Global Humanitarian Foundation. Despite the losses, I feel that it has been a beautiful year. Yes, Liz, we can look beyond death. Today my cousin showed me the way. His brain metastasis has returned and likely there is only a small chance it may be treatable. Yet instead of focusing on the non-possible he always looked, and keeps on looking, at the possible. A very valuable example as it shows, in a way very similar to the experience of Darfuri refugees, that life moves on. You get dealt with a shitty card, well, deal with it!

One of the major lessons of this last year.
Maximize what's good, even if it may seem minimal.
Breathe and live the moment.
Dance the dance of life as often as possible.
Sing in the rain, so you get wet.
Talk with kids.
Look at the moon.
Let it all come to you.

The change over the last year has been great.
Setting objectives and achieving them, without procrastinating or desire for the result.
Or, sometimes, just enjoying the ride.
Letting it all come to me. (Example: while I've been doodling around here in Mexico, an opportunity has popped up to work in Cameroon.)

The Journey

Accepting the bliss that life gives. (Being spoiled all over the world by friends of friends.)

So close to us taking off as Phoenixes in the flames.
Reborn
Sounds so heavy
Yet all it is shed
The ballast
It is known in many a culture
Indigenous Mexico has the Feathered Snake
Which in a form eats its own tail.
In an everlasting rejuvenation
Heraclitus's Live of death and die of life.
As the Phoenix arises again
And again from the flames
Is it all possible
That to reach Blizz
Izz
To let go?
Yap
Be
And Utmost
Is a step toward
The state of mind
That matters = That is.

Yes, Liz, let *Be* be our next project

It is as celestial for me to know that straight after this journey to the inner child we can continue with the next ride.

One of the things I do appreciate about the conquistadors is their saying, "Tis not life that matters, but the road."

Our common road is leading to Africa, Asia, and the Americas. Looking to find collaborators all over the world. Those people that combine healing with spirituality and utmost joy with expertise, integrating knowledge with wisdom.

It has been by bliss to meet you Liz.

Let us combine the inner child and create a family of loving givers out there to be the change they want to see in the world.

Remember the bracelet I gave to one of the special kids in Louisville? Well the mantra is chanting in my heart:

Be the change you want to see in the world.

Pain is inevitable, suffering is optional.

No pain, no gain.

Doctor Gazelle,

Parallel to writing our next book, I shall be working on a travelogue. There are so many stories, fables, histories, and confabulations I would love to share with a wider audience. Addressing such issues as humanitarian organizations in Africa, the perceived hopelessness of Africa, and the in-my-mind future of the world: Africa.

A fascinating continent with beautiful people, where in some countries dictators manage to ruin the lives of many. It is in my heart and mind a place of immense potential. To come back again to Swami Vivekananda and paraphrasing: "Africa has taught me a lot about humanity. And I had the opportunity to share skills and knowledge with African brothers and sisters." Knowledge in my mind always flows two ways. In my mind the teacher is the one to be blessed to learn, and perhaps more so than the student. One of life's full-flow circles.

Dear Dr. Roadrunner,

A mighty feat, hehehehe, the website http://www.ashis.org has already had two thousand individual visitors. I swear it was not me visiting from all my friends' computers and laptops. Nothing is impossible. You think I can aim for twenty thousand now? The flow of visitors seems to come and go, but as we discussed before, during the next speaking tour of the USA and Canada I shall be able to refer people easily to my website. Two groups of friends are helping me in pimping up the site. In one version, the site is lovely pink. You would laugh the night away while seeing it. To engage more people, I am asking people well versed in websites how to buff up the interactivity. For sure, I want more cross-posting with similar-minded friends and colleagues. Perhaps an opportunity to leave video questions or written ones. Somehow it is not flowing yet, but I am sure we will find a way. For example, if you look at the statistics, Mexico is now on the way to becoming the second greatest source of visitors to the site, and a member of Dr. Pilli's family has just offered to translate some of the videos in Spanish. He is a student of the film academy in Mexico City. So again, opportunities arise everywhere. Hoping to infect Colombia, Guatemala, and Nicaragua soon as well.

Lizzie,

Looking forward to your reply.

I loved our discussion of your retirement where all the scenarios were reviewed, laughed about, chosen and rejected, retained to eventually end in a mighty "Let us see what the path brings."

Nothing can be planned.

To be flexible is the utmost response to life.

As you said, no missions abroad—then the China earthquake and the Burmese flood, and before you know it Liz is out there again.

I am going to recline my seat and catch a steady three hours of sleep before I have to rush out of the bus and get another ticket that will extend this fourteen-hour journey by another five hours. So far, time is flying.

Writing, looking at the environment, dreaming, entertaining mischievous thoughts. Well, Liz, this is all for tonight …

Over and out.

Playa del Carmen, 11 June 2008

To love fully is to address unresolved issues. Twenty-one hours of bus riding can lead to clarity. To be my utmost self, I have some issues from the past to resolve. All of a sudden this morning I recognized from the splatter or chaos an order, a pattern. Even if the past is as water under the bridge. Somehow there is a molecular memory that makes that to be One.

Fracture lines in the past need to be set, as if they were breaks in living bone. However much I am aware of danger at some levels and can face it down calmly and resolutely, on a personal level it is not all the same. The nearest and dearest have been hurt by my roller-coaster moods and erratic behavior of yonder, and that needs not a quick fix but a lasting solution.

The paradox is that it is easy to love all people that are not blood related, but that the love for blood relatives can hurt so much. What a night, Liz!

I was planning for a two-month mission in Cameroon, then some more work in South Sudan, the setting up of a foundation in the Netherlands. Who to ask and in what position? What are respectively the vision, the mission, the goals, the objectives, the actors, the stage, the media, and the outcome?

Is there a unity of time, space, and persons as the Ancient Greeks so dearly wanted?

Or does the answer come whispering from within, from our common inner child? I can hear that child giggle, Liz, leading me forward. All that is needed is the opening of the heart, and off you are. Find yourself and that unity of time, space, and person. You are the one. Seemingly, the Universe plays a divine game. Some get sidetracked by the marbles, but it is about the game.

The court jester of the Phoenix Global Humanitarian Foundation is happy to report that we have achieved what we set out to do. To learn, to laugh, to cry, to fly, to moan, to groan, to fly, to be high, to be mischievous, to be blissful, to be the utmost we can be, and to be. As if on the yellow brick road.

Utmost

Who are you, Liz? The scared lion? The tin man? The straw man? Dorothy? Or are you Alice? All of the above in one!

As the complexity theory will eventually open up in the hearts and minds of the people in the world. We are much more and less at the same time than the sum of the parts of the whole.

The bus has arrived. Yet I feel our journey is starting over and over again. Standing still, or running?

Perhaps running to stand still.

After all, the only way we can truly observe is with our eyes closed, sitting still under a tree.

A Japanese bloodgood tree, that is.

Tall yet small.

Waiting to reach out to the sun.

And give a shelter

To my beloved.

Squirrel

The Utmost Question
(Truth and Love)

27 June, 2008

My dearest Ashis,

Cicadas singing Nature's love songs. They were everywhere here. Initially, the sounds of the drum-like membranes in their abdomen were deafening. Cicadas come in cycles of thirteen and seventeen years. The little nymphs fall to the ground, bury themselves, and develop and grow underground. When they finally rise up as grown adults, the males make their loud noises to attract the females and the females demurely flutter their wings in response to the mystery of the mating call. Amazing sounds.

Amazing songs. They mate, lay their eggs, and then die.

Is that all that Nature wants us to do? Sing, mate, give birth, then die? Perhaps in human beings it is the spirit that truly allows us to realize the infinity of our lives. That there is no true beginning nor end. That the spirit goes on beyond the physical realm, eternally flowing through the paths of love. Much like the cicadas, we like to sing. We like to tell our story and be heard. We make noise about our purpose, causes, and missions. Then we mate and bond with someone—either physically, emotionally, psychologically, or spiritually—perhaps all of the above. And this bond gives birth to a child, a creative idea, a collaborative project, a song, a book. In our case, *Utmost*.

And then the book comes to an end yet seems not to die. For it gives way to another creative life cycle. It makes room for another baby to arrive while the firstborn matures.

I look back at the last couple of years, and my heart can't help but smile. We have learned a lot, haven't we, Booff? And there is so much more to learn. It is simply exponential. The act of biting the apple of knowledge is redeemed by applying that knowledge to serve and love others.

So now you are resting in Mexico and enjoying your experiences in Cuba. Yet I know the meaning of feeling complacent. That comfort zone that tends to allow us to hibernate for a time, so we can be revived for more action. To rest and replenish is necessary and healthy. To feel complacency is my sign that I'm ready to prepare to move again, toward a new experience.

What have I learned so far in cowriting *Utmost* with you?

That it is all about giving my maximum to Love and Truth each moment of our lives. That there is a faithful surrender to an inner and higher Source that calls us to do what may seem to be humanly impossible. And that all things are made possible by love. And that you and I are in each other's life for a reason, Ashis. And we know this. And we try to discern what that may be. And we are learning that the reason is simply that moment-to-moment soul connection, which we may be unable to explain on a human level. It's a bond that Destiny created in a most playful and lovable way, to magnify the love that we can radiate to our world. Our love creates in our imagination, and in our reality, the idea that the world is our backyard. Our playground. And there are no true fences around this playground. It is that love that allows us to believe that all is possible and never-ending. For our hope is that the pure essence of this book is passed on down to people of all ages. *Utmost* is our way of giving and sharing with the world what we have learned in these beautiful lives of ours across time and space. It is the symbol of our childlike nakedness, that innocent vulnerability in our humanity that remains to be the pearl of our souls. For as we humans live our lives, we tend to encircle ourselves with steely armors that at times make us lose connection to the true core of our hearts. Our ability to love unconditionally.

Booff, it has been blizz with you indeed.

In a world filled with cataclysms and disasters, when I think of all that we have done together during the last two years, everything in my mind turns into rays of light. That high spiritual voltage that we share is undeniable. And many times, we get overwhelmed. And sometimes we merge into the sublime experience of being in our zone. It is that emotional electricity and wild chemistry we have observed when we dance, when we play, when we laugh, when we eat, when we are quiet. I accept that all now even more. And smile. I smile because the last two years happened. And because there is so much more to come. And because I met you.

Utmost

Ashis, I too secretly prayed for a soul mate. One who would have a similar heart to do the call. And there you are. And like you, I didn't have to do any penance either. I think that's because within the hearts of soul mates, the idea of reward and penance may not exist. Because everything that has to with the soul is a mystery and indefinable, and any attempt to absolutely define something will only limit it. We also talked about the idea that there can be many soul mates in a lifetime. Each soul mate is there for a special purpose in our lives. Perhaps soul mates are there to help us grow spiritually so we can radiate more love to the world.

Having known you, I have discovered even more that we can just be, and just love ... to our utmost.

And my dearest Ashis, Dr. Rainbow, Mr. Blowfish, Dr. Boo-fallo, though I know that it is best to focus on loving others, the very human in me can't help but ask you this ...

To the soul who somehow sees the beauty in me in my worst and most unlovable of times; to my eternal playmate; to my part-ner in exploration and truth to prevent spiritual casualties; to my global missions companion; to my dance-'til-we-drop partner; to my Free Hugs campaign hugger; to my coauthor and confidante; to the man who unselfishly shares his Mom MoonbowGlow with me; to my love and truth friend 'til the end. You have been a di-vine gift in my life. And I am forever grateful for you.

So here is my utmost question:

Would you take a bullet for me, Booff?

The Utmost Question (Truth and Love)

Cancun–Mexico City, 29 June 2008

Dear Liz,

The journey continues. Colombia is next on the schedule. A friend of mine jokingly asked if I ever felt the need to return to work. The Internet connection faltered before I could reply, but the answer is really simple. To continue life's journey every single day, to labor for love, to give self without looking for rewards but the smiles of the children—that is what I do. The desire to go back to Africa is burning, but I want to be fully rested. The next months and years will be packed with projects, books, talking tours, a new not-for-profit organization, and networking with many people with a similar mindset. To unite service, spirituality, healing, and medicine so the vulnerable in the world can start uplifting themselves.

As that aim goes against the social order in the world, sometimes it means to expose oneself to harm's way. Like our driver in Chad who got shot in the liver, lung, and leg during a robbery. It was a matter of minutes, and two emergency flights to the French Military Base, but my friend Goni survived. The French surgeon who saved him I hold in high regard.

After this real-life exposure to the terrible impact of violence, many thoughts crossed my mind. Working in the north of Chad had led to being present at several aerial bombardments, gunshots whizzing by on many occasions, a pitched battle at only thirty kilometers from our homes and five kilometers from the refugee camp, leading to the wounding of over 135 young soldiers, several armed robberies of cars, a break-in and hostage-taking in our compound until we handed over the keys to the pickup.

Yes, friends have been shot, threatened, I have been beaten and robbed. Yet the question "Is it worth it to put your life at risk?" is a no-brainer.

Take one look at the smiles of our friends the refugees and the answer is clear: yes I do accept that bullets may come my way again, and yes, I will take a bullet when it is about protecting something pure and innocent. So given that you are pure and innocent Dr. Gazelle, Dr. Roadrunner, Liz, I will take that bullet.

And my wish is to continue *Utmost* in *Be*!

Afterthoughts

Dear readers,

We are very grateful for your kind attention in reading our book. Our hope is that after reading our book, you get in touch with your gentle spark of deep compassion to make a difference in our world. You already have it in you, waiting for you to put your love into action every moment of your life. It is in that same spark that we find that ability within us to give our Utmost. As we become aware of the needs of those who suffer, we become even more aware of our strengths, talents, and capabilities which we can use to serve and help others. Living our lives with passion and empathy is an incredible way to nurture our compassion within. In my coffee table book *Your Compassionate Nature* I wrote that "Compassion is Love's passion." Each one of us has it in us to choose to live our lives with love and compassion to the fullest.

As we give of ourselves, we end up receiving the best of what life is about.

What has happened after we finished writing *Utmost*?

I had been the chief medical officer of the child psychiatric services at one of the largest comprehensive mental health organization in the USA, in Louisville, Kentucky. Seven Counties Services, Inc. is a role-model in our field in terms of how a non-profit organization can help a community on a grassroots level. What I learned from our organization, I have applied and taught in many parts of the world. I honor our Seven Counties Services, Inc. leadership and staff for all they have taught me, most especially the meaning of mission and service. My profound thanks to Dr. Howard Bracco, our wise and compassionate CEO, Dean Johnson, our bright and creative vice-president of community relations, my steadfast and dedicated fellow psychiatrists and therapists, our incredible staff, and most of all, the astounding people who trusted me to be their physician/psychiatrist.

In May, I founded and chaired a 501 © 3 non-profit organization: Phoenix Global Humanitarian Foundation. (http://www. PGHF.org). Presently, Dr. Renee Campbell, a very dedicated and compassionate humanitarian, is the CEO and chair of PGHF. Dr. Campbell believes in the empowerment of people and those who feel they have no voice. The PGHF mission is to serve those who suffer from disasters, losses, and tragedies. We are now in the midst of partnering with several grassroots organizations in various parts of the world and currently focusing on Uganda, Pine Ridge reservation in South Dakota, and the Philippines. In PGHF, we believe in community empowerment at the grassroots level, alleviating the suffering of those who require basic needs, and to serve those who are isolated because of mental illness, chemical dependency, and incarceration. We also hope to serve those who suffer from physical illnesses like HIV-AIDS, and waterborne illnesses, which cause much suffering to people. Education, relief work, and volunteerism are the basis of our main projects in carrying out our mission. You can access us in our website **PGHF.org, Facebook, NetworkforGood.com, Guidestar.com, Goodsearch.com.**

Dr. Ashis Brahma and I have also started to write another book called *Be.* I have also written another book with Byron Laursen entitled *The Courage to Encourage* and am finishing up another book called *The Phoenix Miracle.* Both should come out at the end of this year or next year. A series of children's books to help children and families who suffer disasters will also be on its way for publishing. There is a lot to be done for our world. Together, we can make a beautiful difference in making our world a better place each day.

The following are websites to explore:

Http://www.PGHF.org
http://www.SevenCounties.org
Http://www.GarciaGray.com
Http;//www.Ashis.org
Http://www.FIMRC.org
Http://www.Forge.org
Http://www.HODR.org
Http://www.NativeProgress.org
Http://www.networkforgood.com
Http://www.facebook.com/causes
Http://www.StopGenocide.org

Http://www.Waterfortheworld.org
Http://www.Dropinthebucket.org
Http://www.TheIRC.org
Http://www.DoctorsWithoutBorders.org
Http://www.WorldVision.org
Http://www.UNHCR.org
Http://www.UNICEF.org
Http://www.IMCWorldwide.org
Http://www.GlobalServiceCorps.org
Http://www.ThailandServiceCorps.org
Http://www.DailyAppreciations.org
Http://www.razoo.com
Http://www.CraftsforPeace.com
Http://www.OWBKY.com/Uganda/rhcf/index.html

A final Afterthought from Dr. Ashis Brahma:
Kampala, Uganda, April 8, 2009

Dear Liz,

Eagles soar in the sky. Mini buses in droves. Small motor bikes weaving through the traffic. Bright, dazzling colors. Big smiles. A claxon, sound systems cranking out music. Here I am sitting in the heart of Kampala, capital of Uganda.

Over the last 12 months I have travelled extensively through North-South America and Europe. It has been a week now in Africa and I am happy I am home. It is my choice to put my feet steady on the ground for a while. Build a house. Help the new organization Phoenix Global Humanitarian Foundation flourish.

Afterthoughts

Have a place to receive friends. So many have offered their houses to me. Let us await the flood of Africa lovers, young and old.

It is homecoming for me as I have made many contacts in previous visits. My thoughts about the process of writing this book are still unchanged. It was a blessing. A blessing to be shared with many. As I finish these afterthoughts I focus on the here and now. The book speaks for itself.

See you soon,

Truth ya Roadrunner